JN017241

宮沢賢治
原文英訳シリーズ2

『セロ弾きのゴーシュ』と 『注文の多い料理店』を 英語で読む

収録作品

『セロ弾きのゴーシュ』
『注文の多い料理店』
『グスコーブドリの伝記』
『雨ニモマケズ』

コスモピア

はじめに

再評価が待たれる革命的な社会思想家、宮沢賢治

　宮沢賢治は、その全身で世界に迫る巨大な戦いの気配を感じていました。この戦いは、地球上のすべての人間を巻き込もうとしたものでした。

　私たちが、賢治が百年前に見たビジョンの重要性を認識し始めたのは、第二次世界大戦が終わってからのことです。1962年に『沈黙の春』を出版したレイチェル・カーソンがその重要性の認識をしたひとりです。彼女はこの本の中で、人間が大気、土地、水を汚染することの重大性について警告しています。その結果、地球環境を守るための法律が多くの国で制定されました。

　さらにその後、動物に対する人間の残酷さが社会問題として明らかになりました。動物にとって最も残酷で非人道的な敵である人間から動物を守るために、法律が制定された国も出てきました。2008年、スペインの議会は、類人猿の権利を尊重することを発表したのです。この権利には、動物があらゆる拷問から解放された生活を送る自由も含まれています。スペインは、人間以外の動物に権利を認めた初めての国になりました。

　動物に対する人間の残酷さは、賢治の最大の関心事であり、『注文の多い料理店』のメインテーマでもあります。私たちは動物を殺すのが得意で、それも賢治の時代よりずっと巧みで計画的になっています。賢治は、彼と同時代の人たちとはズレていたかもしれませんが、自然破壊に反発している現代の私たちとは完全に歩調があっています。つまり、宮沢賢治は私たちと同時代の作家なのです。

　人間が地球を劣化させ破壊していることは、あらゆる領域、あらゆる

レベルで続いています。炭素の排出によって、地球の気温は上がり、気候は不安定になりました。それは、食糧生産と国土の居住性に大きな影響を与えようとしています。また、人間による暴力的な植物や動物の破壊は、数え切れないほどの種の絶滅を招きました。私たちは今、巨大な波の頂点に立っているのですが、徐々にその崩れ落ちていく波による破壊は進んでいます。この波は、私たちが持っているものすべてを押し流し、私たち自身の人生の持続可能性を洗い流してしまうかもしれません。

賢治は、その人生と著作の中で、次の3つを強く願いました。

第一に、地球の自然の恵みを、一時的な利益のために利用するのではなく、育んでいくこと。

第二に、動物に優しく、動物に敬意を払うこと。

第三に、人のために人生を捧げ、悲しみや怒りの重荷を自分のものとして引き受けること。そうすることで、被害を受けた人の重荷を軽減し、無効化することができるからです。

私の親しい友人で劇作家・小説家の井上ひさしが、「100年後も広く読まれる20世紀の日本の作家は、宮沢賢治だけだ」と私に言ったことがあります。

賢治は、奇才の童話作家として何世代にもわたって日本人に愛されてきましたが、革命的な社会思想家であったという点ではあまり評価されてはいません。

将来、宮沢賢治のもつ価値が認められることによって、彼が世界中で不滅の名声を得ることを私は心から願っています。

2023年6月
ロジャー・パルバース
Roger Pulvers

目次

『セロ弾きのゴーシュ』
Gauche the Cellist

読むまえに──
宮沢賢治──もう一人の自分

内気で孤独、そして不器用なチェロ奏者ゴーシュのもとに、猫、かっこう、小狸、そして野ねずみが次々に現れる。彼らとのやりとりを通して、ゴーシュの演奏はどのように変わっていったのだろうか。

『注文の多い料理店』
The Restaurant of Many Orders

読むまえに──
賢治の明確な社会的ビジョン

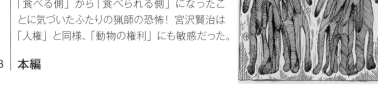

「食べる側」から「食べられる側」になったことに気づいたふたりの猟師の恐怖！ 宮沢賢治は「人権」と同様、「動物の権利」にも敏感だった。

イラスト：ルーシー・パルバース

本書の宮沢賢治の原作はちくま文庫の「宮沢賢治全集」を底本としています。
その上で、『セロ弾きのゴーシュ』『注文の多い料理店』『グスコーブドリの伝記』の3編については新仮名遣いに変更するとともに一部の漢字を変更しています。
韻文である『雨ニモマケズ』に関しては、底本のまま旧仮名遣いで掲載しています。

音声ダウンロードの方法

音声をスマートフォンや PC で、簡単に
聞くことができます。

方法1 スマホで聞く場合

面倒な手続きなしにストリーミング再生で聞くことができます。

※ストリーミング再生になりますので、通信制限などにご注意ください。
　また、インターネット環境がない状況でのオフライン再生はできません。

このサイトにアクセスするだけ！

↳ https://soundcloud.com/yqgfmv3ztp15/
sets/ouon4flobkuu

❶
上記サイトに**アクセス！**

❷ アプリを使う場合は
SoundCloud に
アカウント登録（無料）

方法2 パソコンで音声ダウンロードする場合

パソコンで mp3 音声をダウンロードして、スマホなどに取り込むこと
も可能です。

（スマホなどへの取り込み方法はデバイスによって異なります）

❶ 下記のサイトにアクセス

https://www.cosmopier.com/
download/4864541978

❷ 中央のボタンをクリックする

音声は PC の一括ダウンロード用圧縮ファイル（ZIP 形式）でご提供します。
解凍してお使いください。

音声ファイル表

タイトルと本文は同じ音声ファイルの中に収録されています。

電子版の使い方

音声ダウンロード不要
ワンクリックで音声再生！

本書購読者は
無料でご使用いただけます！
音声付きで
本書がそのままスマホでも
読めます。

電子版ダウンロードには
クーポンコードが必要です

詳しい手順は下記をご覧ください。
右下の QR コードからもアクセスが
可能です。

電子版：無料引き換えコード
H8t7Wg

ブラウザベース（HTML5 形式）でご利用
いただけます。

★クラウドサーカス社 ActiBook 電子書籍
（音声付き）です。

●対応機種
・PC（Windows/Mac）・iOS（iPhone/iPad）
・Android（タブレット、スマートフォン）

電子版ご利用の手順

❶ コスモピア・オンラインショップにアクセス
してください。（無料ですが、会員登録が必要です）

https://www.cosmopier.net/

❷ ログイン後、カテゴリ「電子版」のサブカテゴリ「書籍」をクリックして
ください。

❸ 本書のタイトルをクリックし、「カートに入れる」をクリックしてください。

❹「カートへ進む」→「レジに進む」と進み、「クーポンを変更する」をクリック。

❺「クーポン」欄に本ページにある無料引き換えコードを入力し、「登録する」を
クリックしてください。

❻ 0 円になったのを確認して、「注文する」をクリックしてください。

❼ ご注文を完了すると、「マイページ」に電子書籍が登録されます。

宮沢賢治　略年譜

1896年〈明治29年〉8月　岩手県現在の花巻市に生まれる

1909年（明治42年）4月、岩手県立盛岡中学校に入学

1914年（大正3年）3月、盛岡中学卒業

1915年（大正4年）4月、盛岡高等農林学校入学

1917年（大正6年）同人誌『アザリア』を発行

1918年（大正7年）農学校を卒業。研究生として残る

1920年（大正9年）5月、農林学校研究生を卒業。法華宗系在家仏教団体、国柱会に入信

1921年（大正10年）東京に出奔するも地元に戻り、稗貫郡立稗貫農学校（翌年、花巻農学校に）の教諭に

1922年（大正11年）11月27日妹のトシ死去。『永訣の朝』

1924年（大正13年）『春と修羅』を自費出版。『銀河鉄道の夜』に着手。短編集『注文の多い料理店』を刊行

1926年（大正15年）花巻農学校を依願退職。その後も農業指導などに関わる。チェロを購入

1928年（昭和3年）肺浸潤の診断をうける。その後、一時回復するも病臥生活に

1931年（昭和6年）『雨ニモマケズ』

1932年（昭和7年）雑誌『児童文学』2号に『グスコーブドリの伝記』を発表

1933年〈昭和8年〉9月21日死去

1934年（昭和9年）死後、『銀河鉄道の夜』刊行、『セロ弾きのゴーシュ』発表

セロ弾きのゴーシュ
Gauche the Cellist

イラスト：ルーシー・バルバース

Gauche the Cellist を読むまえに

宮沢賢治—もう一人の自分

内気で孤独で自信のないキャラクターは賢治の作品にたびたび登場します。彼らは純粋無垢であるゆえに相手の本音を読み取れず、誤解されることに悩みます。賢治が愛され続けている理由は、このような人物像に同情し、共感する読者が多いからかもしれません。

🔊 **2**　p.10 /14-52

　賢治の故郷である岩手県花巻市にある宮沢賢治記念館には、賢治のチェロのレプリカが常設展示されています。賢治自身は、どちらかというと不出来な音楽家であったようです。ゴーシュのキャラクターは、フランス語と英語で「不器用な」という意味の「gauche」に由来しており、ゴーシュはどこか作者の鏡のような存在であることに間違いはないでしょう。ゴーシュが背負う「巨きな黒いもの」は、賢治がチェロと弓を購入したとき一緒に手に入れた木製のチェロケースに似ています。

　賢治にとって音楽は、孤独を癒し、不安を解消し、精神を高揚させるものでした。ゴーシュは、動物という形で訪れる自然と、音楽的に交感します。そして、その動物たちは、ゴーシュに自分自身を信じることを促し、観客の前で演奏する勇気を与えてくれるのです。

　内気で孤独で自信のない少年や青年というキャラクターは、賢治の作品によく見られるもので、『銀河鉄道の夜』のジョバンニはその代表的な例です。賢治は、彼の最も有名な詩「雨ニモマケズ」を読めばわかるように、「デクノボー」と呼ばれることや、人に相手にされないことを嫌がりません。彼はむしろ、「サウイフモノ（そういう人）」を目指しています。このような少年や青年のキャラクターは、しばしば純真無垢な存在です。そのため、相手の本音を読み取ることができず、誤解されることに悩みます。賢治が愛され続けている理由のひとつは、このような人物像に同情し、共感する読者が多いからではないでしょうか。

　賢治の作品には、このような人物像に似た行動をする動物もいます。『フランドン農学校の豚』の豚や『オツベルと象』の象に見られるごとく、子どものような世界観が描かれています。賢治の世界には、人間と動物の隙間のない一体感が現れています。どちらかといえば、動物のほうが

賢いともいえるでしょう。賢治の世界では、人間が動物から学ぶべきことがたくさんあるのです。

　現在、多くの生物学者が発見していることですが、私たちが「知性」と呼んでいるものは、人間の能力に限ったものではありません。将来、賢治の登場人物のように、動物たちとコミュニケーションがとれるようになったとき、私たちは皆、同じ船に乗っていることに気づくでしょう。その船とは、絶え間なく、「風景やみんなといつしよにせはしくせはしく明滅しながら」(『春と修羅 序』)時空を航行する地球なのです。

　私が賢治の翻訳をするときには、使う英語の単語の響きを常に意識しています。賢治の散文は、詩と同じように、一種独特な音色をもっています。その意味で、彼の物語は散文詩です。私はそのひとつである『ざしき童子のはなし』を、イギリスのブラッドアックス・ブックスから"Strong in the Rain"というタイトルで出版した賢治の詩の翻訳集に含めました。この色彩豊かな言葉の響きを翻訳から取り除くと、彼の日本語のスタイルを真似ただけの、印象の淡い味気ない、無味乾燥なものになってしまいます。

　狸の子は、ゴーシュに『愉快な馬車屋』を弾くように頼みます。今までこの曲は特定されていませんでした。しかし私はこの曲は、20世紀初頭に作曲家ステファン・イワノビッチ・シャトフがサンクトペテルブルグで発表した「ヴェソーリイ・ヤムシチック」というロシアの曲であると信じています。賢治はロシア的なものに強い関心を持っており、しばしばロシアに言及します。シャトフのコミックソングは、1890年創業のフランスのパテ・レコード社製のレコードとして広く発売されていました。

　イギリスの植民地時代の歌"Hunting Tigers out in Indiah"を賢治が知っていたとは驚きですが、彼はあらゆる音楽を愛し、当時の岩手県内では最も数多くのレコードを集めていたとも言われています。

　猫が頼んだ「印度の虎狩」は、イギリスの大物ハンターが虎を仕留めに行く話です。その歌詞の中にこんな一節があります。「フォークとナプキンで何匹のトラを見つけられるか」。この曲はイギリス人のハンターを主人公にしたもので、トラの「テーブルマナー」、あるいはその欠如について言及されていることから、私はこの曲が『注文の多い料理店』のインスピレーションになったのではないかとさえ思っています。

　ちなみに、India（「印度」）の綴りの最後にhがついてIndiahとしているのは、イギリス人の上品な発音を表しています。イギリス帝国時代の猟師たちは自己顕示欲のために、動物とライフルで戦うことで自分の「男らしさ」を証明しようとするのです。

　賢治は、このような貪欲で無知で因業な殺し屋に同情はしないのです。

It was Gauche's job to play the cello at the cinema in town. Even so, people did not think much of his playing. One could go farther and say that he was the least talented of all the musicians in the orchestra, and because of this he was given a very hard time by the conductor.

One afternoon all the musicians were sitting in a circle rehearsing the Sixth Symphony for the town's upcoming concert. The trumpets were going full blast. The violins were singing out in breezy harmony. The clarinets were tooting away, backing everyone up.

As for Gauche, he just stared at the notes with his lips pursed shut and his eyes like saucers, playing as if his life depended on it.

Without warning, the conductor clapped his hands sharply, and all the musicians stopped playing immediately. A hush fell over the orchestra.

"The cello's coming in late. To-tete tete-ti. Take it from here. Now!"

The musicians all started up again from the place just before they stopped. As for Gauche, blushing beet red and sweating bullets on his brow, he somehow managed to make his way through the part indicated by the conductor. But just as Gauche was getting into it and heaving sighs of relief, the conductor once again clapped his hands sharply.

"Cello! You're out of tune. What's gotten into you, eh? You think I've got time to go through your scales with you, do you?!"

All the other musicians, pitying Gauche, peered deliberately into their notes and tapped or fiddled with their instruments. Gauche frantically tuned his cello. There's no excusing Gauche for his playing, but the cello itself was equally to blame.

Sixth Symphony 「第六交響曲」。ベートーヴェンの交響曲第六番『田園』のことだといわれている

in breezy harmony 「二いろ風のように」。breezy には「朗らかで生き生きとした」という意味と風のようにというふたつの意味がある

tooting away 「ボーボーと」(toot: ラッパや笛などをブップーと吹き鳴らすこと)

with his lips pursed shut 「口をりんと結んで」

hush 静けさ、静寂

fiddled with... 〜をいじった、〜に無意識に触った。fiddle には「ヴァイオリン」という意味もあり、ここでは「楽器を弾く」という意味にもなる

ゴーシュは町の活動写真館でセロを弾く係りでした。けれどもあんまり上手でないという評判でした。上手でないどころではなく実は仲間の楽手のなかではいちばん下手でしたから、いつでも楽長にいじめられるのでした。

ひるすぎみんなは楽屋に円くならんで今度の町の音楽会へ出す第六交響曲の練習をしていました。

トランペットは一生けん命歌っています。

ヴァイオリンも二いろ風のように鳴っています。

クラリネットもボーボーとそれに手伝っています。

ゴーシュも口をりんと結んで眼を皿のようにして楽譜を見つめながらもう一心に弾いています。

にわかにぱたっと楽長が両手を鳴らしました。みんなぴたりと曲をやめてしんとしました。楽長がどなりました。

「セロがおくれた。トォテテ　テテテイ、ここからやり直し。はいっ。」

みんなは今の所の少し前の所からやり直しました。ゴーシュは顔をまっ赤にして額に汗を出しながらやっといま言われたところを通りました。ほっと安心しながら、つづけて弾いていますと楽長がまた手をぱっと拍ちました。

「セロっ。糸が合わない。困るなあ。ぼくはきみにドレミファを教えてまでいるひまはないんだがなあ。」

みんなは気の毒そうにしてわざとじぶんの譜をのぞき込んだりじぶんの楽器をはじいて見たりしています。ゴーシュはあわてて糸を直しました。これはじつはゴーシュも悪いのですがセロもずいぶん悪いのでした。

"Take it from the previous bar. Now!"

They all started up again. Gauche twisted his lips, throwing himself into his playing. Everyone was getting through it quite well and Gauche, too, thought things were going smoothly, when the conductor scared the daylights out of them with another sharp clap of his hands. Gauche was sure he was going to get it again but was thankful that this time the conductor had his eye on someone else. Gauche did exactly what the others had done before, namely stick his nose into his notes pretending to be mulling something over.

"So, take up from where you left off. Now!"

No sooner had they started up again when the conductor suddenly stamped his foot down.

"It won't do!" he hollered. "You call that music? This part is the heart of the piece. It sounds like a racket the way you're playing it. My friends, we have a mere ten days left before the concert. If we professional musicians sound no better than a bunch of blacksmiths banging their anvils or a band of shop boys working in a candy store how can we hold up our head in public, eh?"

"You, Gauche!" he continued. "You're a real problem, you know that? Your playing totally lacks expression. Anger ... joy ... there's not one iota of any emotion in it. If that weren't bad enough, you're just not in sync with the others. You're always steps behind them, coming in after them as if you were tripping on your shoelaces or something. It won't do. Get your act together, will you? I feel sorry for everyone here if our shining Venus Orchestra is badly received solely on your account. So, we'll end the rehearsal here today. Have a rest and make sure you're in the pit at six on the dot."

「今の前の小節から。はいっ。」

みんなはまたはじめました。ゴーシュも口をまげて一生けん命です。そしてこんどはかなり進みました。いいあんばいだと思っていると楽長がおどすような形をしてまたぱたっと手を拍ちました。またかとゴーシュはどきっとしましたがありがたいことにはこんどは別の人でした。ゴーシュはそこでさっきじぶんのときみんながしたようにわざとじぶんの譜へ眼を近づけて何か考えるふりをしていました。

「ではすぐ今の次。はいっ。」

そらと思って弾き出したかと思うといきなり楽長が足をどんと踏んでどなり出しました。

「だめだ。まるでなっていない。このへんは曲の心臓なんだ。それがこんながさがさしたことで。諸君。演奏までもうあと十日しかないんだよ。音楽を専門にやっているぼくらがあの金沓鍛治だの砂糖屋の丁稚なんかの寄り集りに負けてしまったらいったいわれわれの面目はどうなるんだ。おいゴーシュ君。君には困るんだがなあ。表情ということがまるでできてない。怒るも喜ぶも感情というものがさっぱり出ないんだ。それにどうしてもぴたっと外の楽器と合わないもなあ。いつでもきみだけとけた靴のひもを引きずってみんなのあとをついてあるくようなんだ、困るよ、しっかりしてくれないとねえ。光輝あるわが金星音楽団がきみ一人のために悪評をとるようなことでは、みんなへもまったく気の毒だからな。では今日は練習はここまで、休んで六時にはかっきりボックスへ入ってくれ給え。」

They all bowed, stuck cigarettes in their mouth, lit up and left the hall. As for Gauche, he carried his humble cello to a wall. He faced the wall and, pursing his lips to one side, cried like a baby. But he pulled himself together and calmly began to play the part they had been rehearsing all by himself.

Late that night, Gauche returned to his house carrying something big and black on his back. This "house" was really a rundown watermill sitting beside a river on the outskirts of town. Gauche lived there alone. In the mornings he pruned the tomato plants in a small field that surrounded his house and picked insects off the cabbage plants, leaving sometime after noon.

He entered his house, turning on the light, and opened his big black case. It was really no big thing. It was just his scrappy cello. He placed it carefully on the floor, grabbed a glass from the shelf and gulped down some water scooped from a bucket. Then, shaking his head once, he sat in a chair and started to play that day's score with the ferocity of a tiger. Page by page he played and pondered, pondered and played, giving his all till the very end, then returning right back to the beginning, rumbling and roaring his strings.

It was long past midnight when, in the end, he couldn't even tell if it was him playing. His face was as red as a beet, his eyes bloodshot, his expression ferocious. He looked as if, at any moment, he would collapse in a heap.

It was then that someone knocked on the door behind him.

みんなはおじぎをして、それからたばこをくわえてマッチをすったりどこかへ出て行ったりしました。ゴーシュはその粗末な箱みたいなセロをかかえて壁の方へ向いて口をまげてぼろぼろ泪をこぼしましたが、気をとり直してじぶんだけたったひとりいまやったところをはじめからしずかにもいちど弾きはじめました。

その晩遅くゴーシュは何か巨きな黒いものをしょってじぶんの家へ帰ってきました。家といってもそれは町はずれの川ばたにあるこわれた水車小屋で、ゴーシュはそこにたった一人ですんでいて午前は小屋のまわりの小さな畑でトマトの枝をきったり甘藍の虫をひろったりしてひるすぎになるといつも出て行っていたのです。ゴーシュがうちへ入ってあかりをつけるとさっきの黒い包みをあけました。それは何でもない。あの夕方のごつごつしたセロでした。ゴーシュはそれを床の上にそっと置くと、いきなり棚からコップをとってバケツの水をごくごくのみました。

それから頭を一つふって椅子へかけるとまるで虎みたいな勢でひるの譜を弾きはじめました。譜をめくりながら弾いては考え考えては弾き一生けん命しまいまで行くとまたはじめからなんべんもなんべんもごうごうごうごう弾きつづけました。

夜中もとうにすぎてしまいはもうじぶんが弾いているのかもわからないようになって顔もまっ赤になり眼もまるで血走ってとても物凄い顔つきになりいまにも倒れるかと思うように見えました。

そのとき誰かうしろの扉をとんとんと叩くものがありました。

humble 「粗末な」

rundown 壊れかけた、老朽化した

outskirts of town 「町はずれ」

pruned 切り取った、刈り取った

scrappy 「ごつごつした」。scrappy は、がらくたのという意味と気骨のあるという意味を持つ

gulped down 「ごくごくのみました」

ferocity どう猛性、ものすごさ

played and pondered, pondered and played 「弾いては考え考えては弾き」

giving his all 「一生けん命」、全力を尽くして

ferocious 「とても物凄い」、どう猛な

collapse in a heap ドサリと倒れる

"Hauche, that you?" Gauche cried, half asleep.

But what came slipping through the opening door was a large tortoiseshell cat he had seen before. It appeared to be carrying heavy half-ripe tomatoes from Gauche's field.

"Oh, that's a load off my back. Not easy to haul these around."

"What's the meaning of this?" asked Gauche.

"These're a present for you. Have them," said the tortoiseshell cat.

"Who told you to bring tomatoes, eh?" yelled Gauche, in an ill humor from that day's goings-on. "First of all, I wouldn't touch anything brought here by the likes of you! And besides, those tomatoes are from my field, you know. Outrageous picking ones that are not even ripe yet. So it's you who's been munching away on the stalks and kicking up the plants, eh? Scram, stupid cat!"

"Sir, you'll ruin your health if you get all worked up like that," said the cat, hunching her shoulders, squinting and grinning. "Why don't you play Schumann's Truemerai instead? I'll hear it through for you."

"Such impudence, and from a cat to boot," said Gauche, who couldn't figure out what to do with this cat who was really getting on his nerves.

"Don't stand on ceremony just for me. Go on. You see, sir, I can't get to sleep without listening to your music."

「ホーシュ君か。」ゴーシュはねぼけたように叫びました。ところがすうと扉を押してはいって来たのはいままで五六ぺん見たことのある大きな三毛猫<ruby>三毛猫<rt>み け ねこ</rt></ruby>でした。

ゴーシュの畑からとった半分熟したトマトをさも重そうに持って来てゴーシュの前におろして言いました。

「ああくたびれた。なかなか運搬はひどいやな。」

「何だと」ゴーシュがききました。

「これおみやです。たべてください。」三毛猫が言いました。

ゴーシュはひるからのむしゃくしゃを一ぺんにどなりつけました。

「誰がきさまにトマトなど持ってこいと言った。第一おれがきさまらのもってきたものなど食うか。それからそのトマトだっておれの畑のやつだ。何だ。赤くもならないやつをむしって。いままでもトマトの茎をかじったりけちらしたりしたのはおまえだろう。行ってしまえ。猫め。」

すると猫は肩をまるくして眼をすぼめてはいましたが口のあたりでにやにやわらって言いました。

「先生、そうお怒りになっちゃ、おからだにさわります。それよりシューマンのトロメライをひいてごらんなさい。きいてあげますから。」

「生意気なことを言うな。猫のくせに。」

セロ弾きはしゃくにさわってこの猫のやつどうしてくれようとしばらく考えました。

「いやご遠慮はありません。どうぞ。わたしはどうも先生の音楽をきかないとねむられないんです。」

"Impudence, impudence, impudence!" roared Gauche, turning a fiery red and stomping his feet like the conductor did that day, but suddenly changing his mind. "All right, I'll play."

God knows why he locked the door, shut the windows and, picking up his cello, turned off the light. The light outside from the waning three-quarter moon shone through half of the room.

"What was that piece again?"

"Truemerei, by Schumann, the Rheumatic ... oh, I mean, the Romantic," said the cat, wiping its mouth clean.

"Okay. Is this how it goes?"

The cellist ripped his handkerchief into strips and stuffed them well into his own ears. Then he began to storm through the score of "Hunting Tigers out in Indiah".

The cat listened for a while with her head cocked, then suddenly blinked her eyes and, in a flash, dashed headlong for the door. She crashed right into it, but it didn't open. So, in a flurry, she let fly a splutter of sparks from her eyes and brow, as if frustrated by failure like never before in her entire life. She made a face as if about to sneeze, tickled by the sparks coming from her whiskers and nose, then, unable to stand it any longer, began to prance about. As for Gauche, he was really into his music now, playing with greater and greater zeal.

"Sir, that's enough, quite enough. I beg of you, please stop. I won't ask you for another thing."

「生意気だ。生意気だ。生意気だ。」

　ゴーシュはすっかりまっ赤になってひるま楽長のしたように足ぶみしてどなりましたがにわかに気を変えて言いました。

「では弾くよ。」

　ゴーシュは何と思ったか扉にかぎをかって窓もみんなしめてしまい、それからセロをとりだしてあかしを消しました。すると外から二十日過ぎの月のひかりが室のなかへ半分ほどはいってきました。

「何をひけと。」

「トロメライ、ロマチックシューマン作曲。」猫は口を拭いて済まして言いました。

「そうか。トロメライというのはこういうのか。」

　セロ弾きは何と思ったかまずはんけちを引きさいてじぶんの耳の穴へぎっしりつめました。それからまるで嵐のような勢で「印度の虎狩」という譜を弾きはじめました。

　すると猫はしばらく首をまげて聞いていましたがいきなりパチパチパチッと眼をしたかと思うとぱっと扉の方へ飛びのきました。そしていきなりどんと扉へからだをぶっつけましたが扉はあきませんでした。猫はさあこれはもう一生一代の失敗をしたという風にあわてだして眼や額からぱちぱち火花を出しました。するとこんどは口のひげからも鼻からも出ましたから猫はくすぐったがってしばらくくしゃみをするような顔をしてそれからまたさあこうしてはいられないぞというようにはせあるきだしました。ゴーシュはすっかり面白くなってますます勢よくやり出しました。

「先生もうたくさんです。たくさんですよ。ご生ですからやめてください。これからもう先生のタクトなんかとりませんから。」

God knows why 「何と思ったか」

waning　欠けていく

Rheumatic　リウマチの

score 「譜」

"Hunting Tigers out in Indiah"「印度の虎狩」。p.13 を参照

in a flash 「ぱっと」

in a flurry 「あわてだして」、慌ただしく

began to prance about 「はせあるきだしました」（prance: 跳ねまわる）

セロ弾きのゴーシュ　23

"Be quiet. I'm just getting to where they catch the tiger."

The cat, in distress, bolted up, circled about and plastered her body to the wall, leaving a trace on it that, for a while, radiated blue. In the end, she ran round and round Gauche like a little sail on a pinwheel.

"Well, then, I'll ease off for you," he said, putting down his bow.

"Sir, something's a bit off with your playing tonight," said the cat, as if nothing had happened up till then.

Once again, the cat's words rubbed the cellist the wrong way.

"Well, well, maybe there's something off with you!" said Gauche, nonchalantly slipping a cigarette between his lips and producing a match. "Stick out your tongue."

The cat thrust out her pointy tongue as if to mock Gauche.

"Oh yes, a bit on the rough side."

Instantly the cellist struck his match on the cat's tongue and lit his cigarette. The cat was so dumbstruck that she twirled her tongue around like a pinwheel, darted toward the front door, banged her head against it, staggered, then banged it again, staggered again, all in the hope of making an escape. As for Gauche, he just stood there enjoying the scene.

"I'll let you out. Just don't ever come here again. Numbskull!"

The cellist opened the door and, faintly smiling, watched the cat dash through the reeds like a gust of wind. After that he slept soundly, without a care in the world.

「だまれ。これから虎をつかまえる所だ。」

猫はくるしがってはねあがってまわったり壁にからだをくっつけたりしましたが壁についたあとはしばらく青くひかるのでした。しまいは猫はまるで風車のようにぐるぐるぐるぐるゴーシュをまわりました。

ゴーシュもすこしぐるぐるして来ましたので、

「さあこれで許してやるぞ」と言いながらようようやめました。

すると猫もけろりとして

「先生、こんやの演奏はどうかしてますね。」と言いました。

セロ弾きはまたぐっとしゃくにさわりましたが何気ない風で巻たばこを一本だして口にくわえそれからマッチを一本とって

「どうだい。工合（ぐあい）をわるくしないかい。舌を出してごらん。」

猫はばかにしたように尖（とが）った長い舌をベロリと出しました。

「ははあ、少し荒れたね。」セロ弾きは言いながらいきなりマッチを舌でシュッとすってじぶんのたばこへつけました。さあ猫は愕（おどろ）いたの何の舌を風車のようにふりまわしながら入り口の扉（と）へ行って頭でどんとぶっつかってはよろよろとしてまた戻って来てどんとぶっつかってはよろよろまた戻って来てまたぶっつかってはよろよろにげみちをこさえようとしました。

ゴーシュはしばらく面白そうに見ていましたが

「出してやるよ。もう来るなよ。ばか。」

セロ弾きは扉をあけて猫が風のように萱（かや）のなかを走って行くのを見てちょっとわらいました。それから、やっとせいせいしたというようにぐっすりねむりました。

---

plastered 「くっつけた」、なでつけた

pinwheel 「風車」

ease off 和らげる、ゆるめる

something's a bit off なにか違う、なにかおかしい

rubbed...the wrong way 〜の感情を逆なでした

nonchalantly 「何気ない風で」、平然と

thrust out 突き出す

as if to mock 「ばかにしたように」

so dumbstruck that... 「愕いたのなんの」、口がきけないほど驚いて

darted 突進した

staggered 「よろよろとして」

Numbskull 「ばか」

reeds 「萱」、葦（ヨシ）

gust of wind 突風

soundly 「ぐっすり」

The next evening, too, Gauche came home carrying the case with his cello. He gulped down his water and started fiddling away. Before he knew it, it was past twelve, then well past one, then past two as well. Losing track of time, of whether he was playing or not, he went rumbling on ... when he heard a tapping noise in the attic.

"Haven't you learned your lesson, cat?"

When Gauche yelled that, a gray bird came scuffling through a hole in the ceiling. It was a cuckoo, perched on his floor.

"Now I've got a bird on my hands! What brings you here, eh?"

"I want to study music under you," said the cuckoo composedly.

"Music?" chuckled Gauche. "All you can sing is 'cuckoo, cuckoo,' isn't it?"

"You may say so, but it's frightfully difficult you know," replied the cuckoo with an earnest air.

"Difficult? All you do is gaggle away, which any birdbrain could do."

"You're very hard on us, you know. There's a big difference between one cuckoo's cuckoo and another cuckoo's cuckoo, if you listen carefully."

"No difference whatsoever."

"It's obvious that you can't tell the difference. We cuckoos can distinguish the calls of ten thousand cuckoos."

"Suit yourself. So, if you're so smart, why did you come to see me in the first place, eh?"

次の晩もゴーシュがまた黒いセロの包みをかついで
帰ってきました。そして水をごくごくのむとそっくりゆ
うべのとおりぐんぐんセロを弾きはじめました。十二時
は間もなく過ぎ一時もすぎ二時もすぎてもゴーシュはま
だやめませんでした。それからもう何時だかもわからず
弾いているかもわからずごうごうやっていますと誰か屋
根裏をこっこっと叩くものがあります。

「猫、まだこりないのか。」

ゴーシュが叫びますといきなり天井の穴からぽろんと
音がして一疋の灰いろの鳥が降りて来ました。床へとまっ
たのを見るとそれはかっこうでした。

「鳥まで来るなんて。何の用だ。」ゴーシュが言いました。

「音楽を教わりたいのです。」

かっこう鳥はすまして言いました。

ゴーシュは笑って

「音楽だと。おまえの歌は、かっこう、かっこうという
だけじゃあないか。」

するとかっこうが大へんまじめに

「ええ、それなんです。けれどもむずかしいですからね
え。」と言いました。

「むずかしいもんか。おまえたちのはたくさん啼くのが
ひどいだけで、なきようは何でもないじゃないか。」

「ところがそれがひどいんです。たとえばかっこうとこ
うなくのとかっこうとこうなくのとでは聞いていてもよ
ほどちがうでしょう。」

「ちがわないね。」

「ではあなたにはわからないんです。わたしらのなかま
ならかっこうと一万言えば一万みんなちがうんです。」

「勝手だよ。そんなにわかってるなら何もおれの処へ来
なくてもいいではないか。」

"You see, I want to be able to sing my scales properly."

"Only fish need scales!"

"Oh no, I've got to get them right before I go to foreign countries."

"Foreign countries? Too cuckoo to even think about."

"Sir, please teach me the scales. I'll sing along with you."

"You're one big pain in the neck, you know that? Okay, I'll play them just three times, then, when I'm done, you get out of my sight."

Gauche readied his cello, strummed its strings to tune them and played a scale.

"Wrong, wrong," said the cuckoo, fluttering his wings in a flurry. "It doesn't go like that at all."

"Pain in the neck, you are. Okay, so you do it."

"This is how it goes."

The cuckoo leaned forward, posed and cuckooed.

"Ridiculous. You call that a scale? You cuckoos wouldn't know a scale from the Sixth Symphony if you heard one."

"That's not true."

"What do you mean not true."

"It's just tricky when there are lots of notes in a row."

scales 「ドレミファ」、音階

Only fish need scales! scale には「音階」の他に「鱗」という意味もあり、洒落を言いながらドレミファを教わりたいという鳥を侮辱している

Foreign countries? Too cuckoo to even think about 「外国もくそもあるか」。 cuckoo には、カッコウの鳴き声の他に「頭がおかしい」や「正気じゃない」という意味もあるため、ここでは「ばからしくて考えるまでもない」という意味になる

You're one big pain in the neck 「うるさいなあ」

strummed （楽器を）つまびいた、「ボロンボロンと」

「ところが私はドレミファを正確にやりたいんです。」

「ドレミファもくそもあるか。」

「ええ、外国へ行く前にぜひ一度いるんです。」

「外国もくそもあるか。」

「先生どうかドレミファを教えてください。わたしはついてうたいますから。」

「うるさいなあ。そら三べんだけ弾いてやるからすんだらさっさと帰るんだぞ。」

ゴーシュはセロを取り上げてボロンボロンと糸を合わせてドレミファソラシドとひきました。するとかっこうはあわてて羽をばたばたしました。

「ちがいます、ちがいます。そんなんでないんです。」

「うるさいなあ。ではおまえやってごらん。」

「こうですよ。」かっこうはからだをまえに曲げてしばらく構えてから

「かっこう」と一つなきました。

「何だい。それがドレミファかい。おまえたちには、それではドレミファも第六交響楽も同じなんだな。」

「それはちがいます。」

「どうちがうんだ。」

「むずかしいのはこれをたくさん続けたのがあるんです。」

"You mean like this?"

The cellist took up his cello again and played a series of cuckoos. The cuckoo was so overjoyed that he joined in loudly with his own cuckoos, leaning forward and singing on and on. Gauche's hands finally started hurting.

"Hey, enough is enough," he said, putting down his bow.

The cuckoo, disappointed, continued to sing on with his eyes slanted upwards, then finally ended with a "cuckoo-koo" and a "cuckoo-koo-koo-koooo."

"All right, birdie," he said, highly strung, "you got what you came for, now beat it."

"I beg of you, please play one more time. Your cuckoos are not bad, they're just slightly off."

"Off? You've got a cheek! Who's the teacher around here anyway, eh? Now, get lost!"

"Please, I beg of you, just once more. Please?"

The cuckoo bowed to Gauche over and over again.

"This is the last time, though," said Gauche, readying his bow.

"Please string it out as long as you can," gasped the cuckoo, bowing his head.

「つまりこうだろう。」セロ弾きはまたセロをとって、かっこうかっこうかっこうかっこうかっこうとつづけてひきました。

するとかっこうはたいへんよろこんで途中からかっこうかっこうかっこうかっこうとついて叫びました。それももう一生けん命からだをまげていつまでも叫ぶのです。

ゴーシュはとうとう手が痛くなって

「こら、いいかげんにしないか。」と言いながらやめました。するとかっこうは残念そうに眼をつりあげてまだしばらくないていましたがやっと

「……かっこうかくうかっかっかっかっか」と言ってやめました。

ゴーシュがすっかりおこってしまって、

「こらとり、もう用が済んだらかえれ」と言いました。

「どうかもういっぺん弾いてください。あなたのはいいようだけれどもすこしちがうんです。」

「何だと、おれがきさまに教わってるんではないんだぞ。帰らんか。」

「どうかたったもう一ぺんおねがいです。どうか。」かっこうは頭を何べんもこんこん下げました。

「ではこれっきりだよ。」

ゴーシュは弓をかまえました。かっこうは「くっ」とひとつ息をして

「ではなるべく永くおねがいいたします。」といってまた一つおじぎをしました。

highly strung 「すっかりおこって」、神経が高ぶって

beat it 「かえれ」、失せろ、あっちへ行け

You've got a cheek! 「何だと」、図々しい、あつかましい

"This is the last straw," said Gauche, forcing a smile.

When he started to play, the cuckoo, leaning forward, cuckooed and cuckooed with his heart and soul. At first Gauche was in absolutely no humor to play, but as he did so, he sensed that the bird's pitch was better than his. The more he played, the more keenly he felt this.

"Humph, if I keep up this ridiculous business I'll turn into a bird myself."

Gauche instantly stopped playing. At that, the cuckoo got all dizzy, as if clunked on the head, and, with a few cuckoos and a final cu-cuc-koo, fell silent.

"What made you stop?" he asked, looking reproachfully at Gauche. "We cuckoos, even the scaredy-cat ones, cry out till blood gurgles from our throat."

"You impudent birdbrain! How long are you going to keep up this stupid act? Just get out of here, will ya? Look, the sun's almost up."

Gauche pointed to the window. The eastern sky was a hazy silver, and pitch-black clouds were racing through it toward the north.

"Well, then, please continue on until sunrise," said the cuckoo, bowing again. "Once more. It won't be long."

「いやになっちまうなあ。」

「いやになっちまうなあ。」ゴーシュはにが笑いしながら弾きはじめました。するとかっこうはまたまるで本気になって「かっこうかっこうかっこう」とからだをまげてじつに一生けん命叫びました。ゴーシュははじめはむしゃくしゃしていましたがいつまでもつづけて弾いているうちにふっと何だかこれは鳥の方がほんとうのドレミファにはまっているかなという気がしてきました。どうも弾けば弾くほどかっこうの方がいいような気がするのでした。

「えいこんなばかなことしていたらおれは鳥になってしまうんじゃないか。」とゴーシュはいきなりぴたりとセロをやめました。

するとかっこうはどしんと頭を叩かれたようにふらふらっとしてそれからまたさっきのように

「かっこうかっこうかっこうかっかっかっかっかっ」と言ってやめました。それから恨めしそうにゴーシュを見て

「なぜやめたんですか。ぼくらならどんな意気地ないやつでものどから血が出るまでは叫ぶんですよ。」と言いました。

「何を生意気な。こんなばかなまねをいつまでしていられるか。もう出て行け。見ろ。夜があけるんじゃないか。」ゴーシュは窓を指さしました。

東のそらがぼうっと銀いろになってそこをまっ黒な雲が北の方へどんどん走っています。

「ではお日さまの出るまでどうぞ。もう一ぺん。ちょっとですから。」

かっこうはまた頭を下げました。

This is the last straw
「いやになっちまうなあ」、もうたくさんだ、我慢の限界だ

in... no humor 「むしゃくしゃして」、不機嫌で

keenly 鋭く、はっきりと

clunked on the head 「どしんと頭を叩かれた」、頭に一撃を受けた

reproachfully 「恨めしそうに」、とがめるように

scaredy-cat 「意気地のないやつ」、臆病者

hazy silver 「ぼうっと銀色」

pitch-black 「まっ黒な」

"Shut your beak! Trying to get away with anything you can, are you? Stupid little bird," said Gauche, stamping his foot against the floor. "If you don't get out, I'll pluck you clean and gobble you up for breakfast."

The startled cuckoo suddenly flew off, making a beeline for the window. But he clunked his head hard on the glass and flopped right down.

"Look at you, birdbrain, flying right into a pane."

Gauche went to open the window, but this window was not one to be opened easily.

While Gauche was rattling the rickety window frame, the cuckoo clunked against the panes and flopped down again. Blood trickled from the base of his beak.

"I'm opening it now, so hold your horses, will ya?"

When Gauche finally managed to open the window about two inches, the cuckoo, in a final desperate effort, with his eyes fixed on the eastern sky beyond the panes of glass, took flight as if it was the last thing he would ever do. But this time he hit a pane even harder, falling to the floor and remaining there, without budging, for some time. When Gauche reached out to grab the cuckoo to help him fly away, the cuckoo suddenly opened his eyes and sprang up, heading straight for the glass again. Gauche found himself raising up his leg and giving the window a swift kick. This shattered two or three panes with a huge crashing sound, and the window, frame and all, dropped to the ground outside.

The cuckoo flew like an arrow out of what remained of the window, and continued to fly straight away, on and on, until, in the end, he could be seen no more.

Gauche, stunned, just stared into the distance, until, after a while, plopping down in a corner of the room and falling dead asleep.

「黙れっ。いい気になって。このばか鳥め。出て行かんとむしって朝飯に食ってしまうぞ。」ゴーシュはどんと床をふみました。

するとかっこうはにわかにびっくりしたようにいきなり窓をめがけて飛び立ちました。そして硝子にはげしく頭をぶっつけてばたっと下へ落ちました。

「何だ、硝子へばかだなあ。」ゴーシュはあわてて立って窓をあけようとしましたが元来この窓はそんなにいつでもするする開く窓ではありませんでした。ゴーシュが窓のわくをしきりにがたがたしているうちにまたかっこうがばっとぶっつかって下へ落ちました。見ると嘴のつけねからすこし血が出ています。

「いまあけてやるから待っていろったら。」ゴーシュがやっと二寸ばかり窓をあけたとき、かっこうは起きあがって何が何でもこんどこそというようにじっと窓の向うの東のそらをみつめて、あらん限りの力をこめた風でぱっと飛びたちました。もちろんこんどは前よりひどく硝子につきあたってかっこうは下へ落ちたまましばらく身動きもしませんでした。つかまえてドアから飛ばしてやろうとゴーシュが手を出しましたらいきなりかっこうは眼をひらいて飛びのきました。そしてまたガラスへ飛びつきそうにするのです。ゴーシュは思わず足を上げて窓をばっとけりました。ガラスは二三枚物すごい音して砕け窓はわくのまま外へ落ちました。そのがらんとなった窓のあとをかっこうが矢のように外へ飛びだしました。そしてもうどこまでもどこまでもまっすぐに飛んで行ってとうとう見えなくなってしまいました。ゴーシュはしばらく呆れたように外を見ていましたが、そのまま倒れるように室のすみへころがって睡ってしまいました。

Shut your beak 「黙れっ」。鳥なので mouth ではなく、beak（クチバシ）となる

Trying to get away with anything you can 「いい気になって」、鳥でも虫がよすぎる

pluck you clean （丸裸になるまで羽を）「むしって」

gobble you up 「食ってしまう」、食べつくす

making a beeline まっすぐ進んで

flopped right down 「ばたっと下へ落ちました」、ドサッと倒れた

pane 「硝子」、窓ガラス

rattling 「がたがたして」

rickety ガタガタの

trickled したたり落ちた

hold your horses 「待っていろ」、落ち着け、ちょっと待て

without budging 身動きもない

stunned 「呆れたように」、啞然として

The next night, Gauche had played his cello until past midnight and, exhausted, was drinking a glass of water when someone started knocking on the door. This time, determined to throw out whoever it was just like he had the cuckoo from the night before, he sat where he was, holding his glass. The door opened a little and a tanuki cub came into his house.

"Hey, tanuki, ever heard of tanuki stew?" barked Gauche, opening the door a bit wider and stamping his foot down.

At that, the tanuki cub, a vacant look in his eyes, sat himself down on the floor.

"Tanuki stew? Haven't a clue," he said, cocking his head as if trying to figure out what it could be.

Gauche felt like bursting into laughter, but he put a scary expression on his face instead.

"I'll tell you, then," he said. "Tanuki stew is made by taking a tanuki like you, mixing it up with cabbage and salt and boiling it before the likes of me wolfs it down."

"But my dad," said the tanuki cub as if mystified, "told me to come here and learn from a really nice man like you, Mr. Gauche."

At that, he really did burst into a laugh this time.

"Learn ... that what he said, eh? Look, I'm a busy man. Besides, I'm sleepy."

"My job's playing the small drum," said the tanuki cub, stepping forward in a sudden burst of energy. "He told me to beat the drum in time with the cello."

"Drum? There's no drum around here."

"Yes there is, here," said the cub, producing two drumsticks from behind his back.

次の晩もゴーシュは夜中すぎまでセロを弾いてつかれて水を一杯のんでいますと、また扉をこつこつ叩くものがあります。

今夜は何が来てもゆうべのかっこうのようにはじめからおどかして追い払ってやろうと思ってコップをもったまま待ち構えて居りますと、扉がすこしあいて一疋の狸の子がはいってきました。ゴーシュはそこでその扉をもう少し広くひらいて置いてどんと足をふんで、

「こら、狸、おまえは狸汁ということを知っているかっ。」とどなりました。すると狸の子はぼんやりした顔をしてきちんと床へ座ったままどうもわからないというように首をまげて考えていましたが、しばらくたって

「狸汁ってぼく知らない。」と言いました。ゴーシュはその顔を見て思わず吹き出そうとしましたが、まだ無理に恐い顔をして、

「では教えてやろう。狸汁というのはな。おまえのような狸をな、キャベジや塩とまぜてくたくたと煮ておれさまの食うようにしたものだ。」と言いました。すると狸の子はまたふしぎそうに

「だってぼくのお父さんがね、ゴーシュさんはとてもいい人でこわくないから行って習えと言ったよ。」と言いました。そこでゴーシュもとうとう笑い出してしまいました。

「何を習えと言ったんだ。おれはいそがしいんじゃないか。それに睡いんだよ。」

狸の子は俄に勢がついたように一足前へ出ました。

「ぼくは小太鼓の係りでねえ。セロへ合わせてもらって来いと言われたんだ。」

「どこにも小太鼓がないじゃないか。」

「そら、これ」狸の子はせなかから棒きれを二本出しました。

throw out 「追い払って」、追い出して、つまみ出して

tanuki cub 「狸の子」

tanuki stew 「狸汁」

vacant look 「ぼんやりとした顔」

Haven't a clue 「ぼく知らない」

wolfs it down 一気に平らげる

as if mystified 「ふしぎそうに」

セロ弾きのゴーシュ　37

"And what do you propose doing with those?"

"Please play 'The Merry Coachman.' Please."

"What's 'The Merry Coachman,' some sort of jazz?"

"Oh, here are the notes," said the cub, bringing a sheet of music from behind his back.

"Boy, this is some weird song," said Gauche, laughing as he took the sheet in his hand. "All right, then, I'll play it. You going to beat a drum, are you?"

Gauche started to play his cello, throwing glances at the tanuki cub, wondering what he was going to do. The cub started to beat time below the bridge of the cello with the two sticks. He wasn't bad at all, and Gauche got drawn into the rhythm as he played. When they had finished playing, the cub stood there for a while, cocking his head in thought.

"Mr. Gauche," he finally said, "it's bizarre but you fall behind when you play the D string. It makes me kind of lose my place."

Gauche was alarmed. No matter how nimbly he played that string, the sound from it was somehow delayed. He had noticed this the night before.

"Hmm, you might be right. Must be the cello's fault," said Gauche, sadly.

The cub was again plunged in thought.

"Wonder what could be the matter with it," he finally said, feeling sorry for Gauche. "Let's give it another go, okay?"

"Fine. Here I go."

Gauche started up again. The tanuki cub tapped out the beat like he did before, from time to time bending his neck to put an ear against the cello. By the time they had finished, the eastern sky was all hazy and bright again.

「それでどうするんだ。」

「ではね、『愉快な馬車屋』を弾いてください。」

「何だ愉快な馬車屋ってジャズか。」

「ああこの譜だよ。」狸の子はせなかからまた一枚の譜をとり出しました。ゴーシュは手にとってわらい出しました。

「ふう、変な曲だなあ。よし、さあ弾くぞ。おまえは小太鼓を叩くのか。」ゴーシュは狸の子がどうするのかと思ってちらちらそっちを見ながら弾きはじめました。

すると狸の子は棒をもってセロの駒の下のところを拍子をとってぽんぽん叩きはじめました。それがなかなかうまいので弾いているうちにゴーシュはこれは面白いぞと思いました。

おしまいまでひいてしまうと狸の子はしばらく首をまげて考えました。

それからやっと考えついたというように言いました。

「ゴーシュさんはこの二番目の糸をひくときはきたいに遅れるねえ。なんだかぼくがつまずくようになるよ。」

ゴーシュははっとしました。たしかにその糸はどんなに手早く弾いてもすこしたってからでないと音が出ないような気がゆうべからしていたのでした。

「いや、そうかもしれない。このセロは悪いんだよ。」とゴーシュはかなしそうに言いました。すると狸は気の毒そうにしてまたしばらく考えていましたが

「どこが悪いんだろうなあ。ではもう一ぺん弾いてくれますか。」

「いいとも弾くよ。」ゴーシュははじめました。狸の子はさっきのようにとんとん叩きながら時々頭をまげてセロに耳をつけるようにしました。そしておしまいまで来たときは今夜もまた東がぼうと明るくなっていました。

"Ah, it's dawning. Thank you very much."

The tanuki cub slung the sheet of music and the sticks onto his back in a great rush, stuck them on with duck tape, bowed a few times and scurried away. Gauche remained where he was in a daze, for a while breathing in the wind from the window broken the day before, then, hoping to get back his strength for the next day in town, slipped under the covers and off to sleep.

The next night, too, gripping his notes and feeling very drowsy from losing himself in playing his cello right through the night until dawn, he heard knocking on his door. Even though the knocking was so faint he could barely hear it, he recognized it as knocking from the previous nights.

"Enter," he said.

A field mouse flitted through a crack in the door with a baby mouse behind her. The baby mouse was no bigger than a pencil eraser, and Gauche found it hard to stifle a smile. The field mouse looked about with googly eyes, as if wondering why Gauche was laughing at her. She came right up to him and pushed a green chestnut toward him.

"Sir, this child is very ill and could die any day," she said, bowing formally. "For mercy's sake, please make him well."

"Who ever said I was a doctor?" said Gauche, a bit miffed.

The mother mouse gazed at the floor in silence.

"Sir, but you are a doctor. I mean, every day you cure everyone's illnesses, don't you?"

「ああ夜が明けたぞ。どうもありがとう。」狸の子は大へんあわてて譜や棒きれをせなかへしょってゴムテープでぱちんととめておじぎを二つ三つすると急いで外へ出て行ってしまいました。

ゴーシュはぼんやりしてしばらくゆうべのこわれたガラスからはいってくる風を吸っていましたが、町へ出て行くまで睡って元気をとり戻そうと急いでねどこへもぐり込みました。

次の晩もゴーシュは夜通しセロを弾いて明方近く思わずつかれて楽器をもったままうとうとしていますとまた誰か扉をこつこつと叩くものがあります。それもまるで聞えるか聞えないかの位でしたが毎晩のことなのでゴーシュはすぐ聞きつけて「おはいり。」と言いました。すると戸のすきまからはいって来たのは一ぴきの野ねずみでした。そして大へんちいさなこどもをつれてちょろちょろとゴーシュの前へ歩いてきました。そのまた野ねずみのこどもと来たらまるでけしごむのくらいしかないのでゴーシュはおもわずわらいました。すると野ねずみは何をわらわれたろうというようにきょろきょろしながらゴーシュの前に来て、青い栗の実を一つぶ前においてちゃんとおじぎをして言いました。

「先生、この児があんばいがわるくて死にそうでございますが先生お慈悲になおしてやってくださいまし。」

「おれが医者などやれるもんか。」ゴーシュはすこしむっとして言いました。すると野ねずみのお母さんは下を向いてしばらくだまっていましたがまた思い切ったように言いました。

「先生、それはうそでございます、先生は毎日あんなに上手にみんなの病気をなおしておいでになるではありませんか。」

slung... onto his back 「〜をせなかへしょって」

duck tape 「ゴムテープ」。duck は「鴨」を意味するため、背中にしょっているイメージを膨らませることができる。

scurried away 「急いで外へ出て行って」、慌てて走り去った

in a daze 「ぼんやりして」

drowsy 「うとうとして」

losing himself in... 〜に没頭して

field mouse 「野ねずみ」

flitted 軽やかに通った

found it hard to stifle a smile 「おもわずわらいました」

looked about with googly eyes 「きょろきょろしながら」

green chestnut 「青い栗の実」

For mercy's sake 「お慈悲に」、後生だから

miffed 「むっとして」

"What sort of nonsense is this?"

"But, sir," she said determinedly, "Granny Rabbit and Papa Tanuki got all better, and you even fixed up the catty horned owl, so it'd be cruel if you couldn't do something for my baby."

"Hey now, there seems to be some mistake here," said Gauche, taken aback. "I've never cured any catty horned owls. And the tanuki cub just came in here last night pretending he was playing in some band or something, got it?"

Gauche smiled down at the baby mouse.

"Oh, this little one should have fallen ill earlier," said the mother mouse, bursting into tears. "Your playing would have cured him. But he got sick just after you stopped, and if you won't play no matter how much I beg and plead, then we'll just have to accept his miserable fate."

"Eh? You mean, my cello playing cured the catty horned owl and the rabbit?" shrieked Gauche in surprise. "What's going on here, eh?"

"That's right," said the field mouse, rubbing her eye with her paw. "All of the creatures around here go under your floorboards to get better whenever they're sick."

"And that cures them?"

"It does. Their circulation improves and they feel great. Some get better right away, while others get better once they're home."

「何のことだかわからんね。」

「だって先生先生のおかげで、兎さんのおばあさんもなおりましたし狸さんのお父さんもなおりましたしあんな意地悪のみみずくまでなおしていただいたのにこの子ばかりお助けをいただけないとはあんまり情ないことでございます。」

「おいおい、それは何かの間ちがいだよ。おれはみみずくの病気なんどなおしてやったことはないからな。もっとも狸の子はゆうべ来て楽隊のまねをして行ったがね。ははん。」ゴーシュは呆れてその子ねずみを見おろしてわらいました。

すると野ねずみのお母さんは泣きだしてしまいました。

「ああこの児はどうせ病気になるならもっと早くなればよかった。さっきまであれ位ごうごうと鳴らしておいでになったのに、病気になるといっしょにぴたっと音がとまってもうあとはいくらおねがいしても鳴らしてくださらないなんて。何てふしあわせな子どもだろう。」

ゴーシュはびっくりして叫びました。

「何だと、ぼくがセロを弾けばみみずくや兎の病気がなおると。どういうわけだ。それは。」

野ねずみは眼を片手でこすりこすり言いました。

「はい、ここらのものは病気になるとみんな先生のおうちの床下にはいって療すのでございます。」

「すると療るのか。」

「はい。からだ中とても血のまわりがよくなって大へんいい気持ですぐに療る方もあればうちへ帰ってから療る方もあります。」

catty 「意地悪の」
horned owl 「みみずく」
taken aback 「呆れて」
plead 「おねがいして」
under your floorboards 「先生のおうちの床下」
circulation 「血のまわり」、血行

"Oh, is that it? You telling me that the sounds from my cello sort of rumble down and your illnesses get better as if they were giving you a massage? Okay, I got it. I'll play for you."

Gauche tightened his strings, then picked up the baby mouse between his fingers and popped him into the hole in the cello.

"I'm going with him," the mother mouse said, frantically making a jump for the cello. "All mothers go to the hospital with their children."

"So you're going in too, are you," said Gauche, trying to get the mother mouse through the hole. But only half her face went in.

"Are you all right in there?" she screamed to her baby in the cello, flapping about. "I've always taught him that when you fall, you fall skillfully with your feet together."

"I'm good," answered the baby mouse from the bottom of the cello in a voice as thin as a mosquito's. "I had a good fall."

"He's fine," said Gauche, looking down at the mother mouse. "So, you don't have to wail away like that."

Then he picked up his bow and scraped away at some rhapsody or something. The mother mouse listened with a worried expression on her face.

"That'll do. Please let him out now," she said, controlling herself.

"Huh? Is that all you want?"

Gauche leaned the cello to one side, placing his hand against the hole. The baby mouse popped right out of the hole. Gauche put him down without saying anything. The baby mouse's eyes were shut tight and he was shivering and shaking like a leaf.

"How was that, eh? Good? How you feeling?"

「ああそうか。おれのセロの音がごうごうひびくと、それがあんまの代りになっておまえたちの病気がなおるというのか。よし。わかったよ。やってやろう。」ゴーシュはちょっとギウギウと糸を合せてそれからいきなりのねずみのこどもをつまんでセロの孔から中へ入れてしまいました。

「わたしもいっしょについて行きます。どこの病院でもそうですから。」おっかさんの野ねずみはきちがいのようになってセロに飛びつきました。

「おまえさんもはいるかね。」セロ弾きはおっかさんの野ねずみをセロの孔からくぐしてやろうとしましたが顔が半分しかはいりませんでした。

野ねずみはばたばたしながら中のこどもに叫びました。

「おまえそこはいいかい。落ちるときいつも教えるように足をそろえてうまく落ちたかい。」

「いい。うまく落ちた。」こどものねずみはまるで蚊のような小さな声でセロの底で返事しました。

「大丈夫さ。だから泣き声出すなというんだ。」ゴーシュはおっかさんのねずみを下におろしてそれから弓をとって何とかラプソディとかいうものをごうごうがあがあ弾きました。するとおっかさんのねずみはいかにも心配そうにその音の工合（ぐあい）をきいていましたがとうとうこらえ切れなくなったふうで

「もう沢山です。どうか出してやってください。」と言いました。

「なあんだ、これでいいのか。」ゴーシュはセロをまげて孔（あな）のところに手をあてて待っていましたら間もなくこどものねずみが出てきました。ゴーシュは、だまってそれをおろしてやりました。見るとすっかり目をつぶってぶるぶるぶるぶるふるえていました。

「どうだったの。いいかい。気分は。」

rumble down 「ごうごうひびく」

frantically 「きちがいのように」、気も狂わんばかりに、必死に

flapping about 「ばたばたしながら」

wail away 「泣き声出す」

scraped away 「ごうごうがあがあ弾きました」

shaking like a leaf （恐怖などで）「ぶるぶるふるえて」

The baby mouse didn't say a word, but just shivered and shook with his eyes shut tight until, in an instant, he stood up and dashed about the floor.

"Oh, he's better," said the mother mouse, running around with her child. "Thank you, thank you."

Then she stood before Gauche and bowed, thanking him profusely. As for Gauche, for some reason he felt quite sorry for them.

"Hey, do you mice eat bread?" he asked.

"No thank you," she said, staring about the room. "I am aware that this bread of yours is made from wheat dough that is kneaded and steamed until it swells all up into something very delicious, but, having said that, we have never once visited your shelves and, besides, how could we presume to take home some of your bread after all you have done for us?"

"No, you've misunderstood. I just wanted to know if you ate bread or not. So, you do eat it. Just a second. I'll give some to your child for his sore tummy."

Gauche laid his cello on the floor, pinched a morsel of bread off a loaf on the shelf and put it in front of them. The mother mouse, beside herself with tears and laughter, bowed to him, put the bread carefully between her teeth and left with her baby in the lead.

"All this talking to mice has really exhausted me."

Gauche collapsed into his bed and, before he knew it, was dead to the world.

こどものねずみはすこしもへんじもしないでまだしばらく眼をつぶったままぶるぶるぶるぶるふるえていましたがにわかに起きあがって走りだした。

　「ああよくなったんだ。ありがとうございます。ありがとうございます。」おっかさんのねずみもいっしょに走っていましたが、まもなくゴーシュの前に来てしきりにおじぎをしながら

　「ありがとうございますありがとうございます」と十ばかり言いました。

　ゴーシュは何がなかあいそうになって

　「おい、おまえたちはパンはたべるのか。」とききました。

　すると野ねずみはびっくりしたようにきょろきょろあたりを見まわしてから

　「いえ、もうおパンというものは小麦の粉をこねたりむしたりしてこしらえたものでふくふく膨らんでいておいしいものなそうでございますが、そうでなくても私どもはおうちの戸棚へなど参ったこともございませんし、ましてこれ位お世話になりながらどうしてそれを運びになんど参れましょう。」と言いました。

　「いや、そのことではないんだ。ただたべるのかときいたんだ。ではたべるんだな。ちょっと待てよ。その腹の悪いこどもへやるからな。」

　ゴーシュはセロを床へ置いて戸棚からパンを一つまみむしって野ねずみの前へ置きました。

　野ねずみはもうまるでばかのようになって泣いたり笑ったりおじぎをしたりしてから大じそうにそれをくわえてこどもをさきに立てて外へ出て行きました。

　「あああ。ねずみと話するのもなかなかつかれるぞ。」ゴーシュはねどこへどっかり倒れてすぐぐうぐうねむってしまいました。

in an instant 「にわかに」、すぐに

profusely 「十ばかり」、やたらと、ふんだんに

morsel 「一つまみ」、（食べ物の）ひと口分、少量

beside herself with... （怒り、喜び、心配などで）我を忘れて

with her baby in the lead 「こどもをさきに立てて」

Then one night, six days later, the musicians of the Venus Orchestra, their faces flushed, left the stage in succession for the waiting room in the town hall, all carrying their instruments. They had stormed through the Sixth Symphony with flying colors, and stormy applause were still thundering in the hall. The conductor made his way lazily among them with his hands in his pockets, as if he couldn't give a fig about the audience's reaction. Actually, he was bursting with delight. The musicians were all lighting up their cigarettes or replacing instruments in their cases.

Applause still rang out in the hall. Far from abating, the applause got louder and louder, until it really sounded like thunder. The emcee for the evening entered with a white ribbon pinned to his chest.

"They're clamoring for an encore. Won't you give them something short?"

"No way," said the conductor brusquely. "After such a stupendous piece, whatever we played would be bound to be a letdown."

"But, won't you just go out and at least have a word to them?" said the emcee to the conductor.

"Out of the question. Hey, Gauche, why don't you play something for them?"

"Me?" said Gauche, flabbergasted.

"Yes, you, you," piped in the first violin, raising his head.

それから六日目の晩でした。金星音楽団の人たちは町の公会堂のホールの裏にある控室へみんなぱっと顔をほてらしてめいめい楽器をもって、ぞろぞろホールの舞台から引きあげて来ました。首尾よく第六交響曲を仕上げたのです。ホールでは拍手の音がまだ嵐のように鳴って居ります。楽長はポケットへ手をつっ込んで拍手なんかどうでもいいというようにのそのそみんなの間を歩きまわっていましたが、じつはどうして嬉しさでいっぱいなのでした。みんなはたばこをくわえてマッチをすったり楽器をケースへ入れたりしました。

　ホールではまだぱちぱち手が鳴っています。それどころではなくいよいよそれが高くなって何だかこわいような手がつけられないような音になりました。大きな白いリボンを胸につけた司会者がはいって来ました。

　「アンコールをやっていますが、何かみじかいものでもきかせてやってくださいませんか。」

　すると楽長がきっとなって答えました。「いけませんな。こういう大物のあとへ何を出したってこっちの気の済むようには行くもんでないんです。」

　「では楽長さん出て一寸挨拶して下さい。」

　「だめだ。おい、ゴーシュ君、何か出て弾いてやってくれ。」

　「わたしがですか。」ゴーシュは呆気にとられました。

　「君だ、君だ。」ヴァイオリンの一番の人がいきなり顔をあげて言いました。

in succession 「ぞろぞろ」、相次いで

with flying colors 「首尾よく」、ものの見事に

couldn't give a fig 「どうでもいい」

Far from abating 「それどころではなく」（abate: 弱まる）

clamoring for... ～を強く要求する

brusquely 「きっとなって」、けんけんと、不愛想に

stupendous 驚異的な

flabbergasted 「呆気にとられ」、仰天して

piped in 言葉をはさんだ、（音楽などを）流した

"C'mon, out you go," said the conductor.

They all made Gauche pick up his cello, then, opening the door, gave him a shove toward the stage. When he got to the stage, feeling all thumbs with his cello in his hands, the audience went even wilder with applause. There were even people who let out shouts. How much humiliation can a man take? Okay, I'll show them all, he thought. I'll play "Hunting Tigers out in Indiah."

Gauche, now perfectly composed, stepped out into the middle of the stage. Then, just like the time the cat visited him, he played the tiger hunting piece with the ferocity and energy of an angry elephant. The audience listened intently, without making a twitter. Gauche continued to make his way through the piece, from the part where the distressed cat sparked off to the part where she incessantly rammed into the door.

When it was all over, Gauche escaped with his cello into the greenroom just like a cat, without looking at anyone. All the musicians, and the conductor too, just sat there in silence, staring straight ahead, like people who had just been through a fire.

As for Gauche, he seemed beyond caring. He walked quickly among them straight to a divan, plopping down into it and crossing his feet. All the musicians turned their gaze on him. They weren't laughing at him at all. In fact, they looked very serious. This is one pretty weird evening, thought Gauche.

The conductor stood in front of him.

「さあ出て行きたまえ。」楽長が言いました。みんなもセロをむりにゴーシュに持たせて扉をあけるといきなり舞台へゴーシュを押し出してしまいました。ゴーシュがその孔のあいたセロをもってじつに困ってしまって舞台へ出るとみんなはそら見ろというように一そうひどく手を叩きました。わあと叫んだものもあるようでした。

「どこまでひとをばかにするんだ。よし見ていろ。印度の虎狩をひいてやるから。」ゴーシュはすっかり落ちついて舞台のまん中へ出ました。

それからあの猫の来たときのようにまるで怒った象のような勢で虎狩りを弾きました。ところが聴衆はしいんとなって一生けん命聞いています。ゴーシュはどんどん弾きました。猫が切ながってぱちぱち火花を出したところも過ぎました。扉へからだを何べんもぶっつけた所も過ぎました。

曲が終るとゴーシュはもうみんなの方などは見もせずちょうどその猫のようにすばやくセロをもって楽屋へ逃げ込みました。すると楽屋では楽長はじめ仲間がみんな火事にでもあったあとのように眼をじっとしてひっそりとすわり込んでいます。ゴーシュはやぶれかぶれだと思ってみんなの間をさっさとあるいて行って向うの長椅子へどっかりとからだをおろして足を組んですわりました。

するとみんなが一ぺんに顔をこっちへ向けてゴーシュを見ましたがやはりまじめでべつにわらっているようでもありませんでした。

「こんやは変な晩だなあ。」

ゴーシュは思いました。ところが楽長は立って言いました。

gave him a shove 「押し出して」

all thumbs 不器用な、ぶざまな、ぎこちない

intently 「一生けん命」、熱心に

distressed 苦しめられた、動揺した

incessantly 「何べんも」、絶え間なく、ひっきりなしに

rammed into 「ぶっつけた」

greenroom 「楽屋」

beyond caring 「やぶれかぶれ」、どうでもよくなる

divan 「長椅子」

"Gauche, you were brilliant. The piece is no masterpiece, but you held our attention wonderfully. You've made great progress in a week or ten days. Ten days ago you were a babe in arms. Today you're a trooper! You really had it in you all along, you did!"

All his colleagues came up to him, saying "Well done."

"You know, he can do it because he's so robust," said the conductor standing behind the musicians. "It would've killed an ordinary human."

It was late that night when Gauche got back home. First he gulped down his water. After that, he opened his window and, gazing into the distant sky where the cuckoo had appeared to fly away, he said ...

"Oh, cuckoo. Please forgive me for what I did. It wasn't out of anger. I promise you that."

「ゴーシュ君、よかったぞお。あんな曲だけれどもここではみんなかなり本気になって聞いてたぞ。一週間か十日の間にずいぶん仕上げたなあ。十日前とくらべたらまるで赤ん坊と兵隊だ。やろうと思えばいつでもやれたんじゃないか、君。」

仲間もみんな立って来て「よかったぜ」とゴーシュに言いました。

「いや、からだが丈夫だからこんなこともできるよ。普通の人なら死んでしまうからな。」楽長が向うで言っていました。

その晩遅くゴーシュは自分のうちへ帰って来ました。

そしてまた水をがぶがぶ呑みました。それから窓をあけていつかかっこうの飛んで行ったと思った遠くのそらをながめながら

「ああかっこう。あのときはすまなかったなあ。おれは怒ったんじゃなかったんだ。」と言いました。

trooper 「兵隊」、がんばり屋

robust 「丈夫」、（人が）たくましい

注文の多い料理店
The Restaurant of Many Orders

イラスト：ルーシー・バルバース

The Restaurant of Many Orders を読むまえに

賢治における明確な社会的ビジョン

「食べる側」から「食べられる側」になったことに気づいたふたりの猟師の恐怖！ 宮沢賢治は「人権」と同様、「動物の権利」にも敏感だった。

　『注文の多い料理店』は、間違いなく、宮沢賢治の最も人気のある物語のひとつです。ユーモアとサスペンスが入り混じったこの作品では、ふたりの不幸な猟師が、山猫軒というレストランのダイニングルームに向かうという終盤の展開があります。

　ふたりは文字通り、そして比喩的に、有利が不利になり、自分たちの立場が「食べる側」から「食べられる側」へと逆転してしまう羽目に陥るのです。

> 「どうもおかしいぜ。」
>
> 「ぼくもおかしいとおもう。」
>
> 「沢山の注文というのは、向うがこっちへ注文してるんだよ。」

(p.73)

　自分たちがメインディッシュであることに気づいて、ふたりは恐怖に震えるのです。

　彼らが通るドアには、

> 　十五分とお待たせはいたしません。すぐたべられます。

(p.73)

と書かれています（この「たべられます」は、英語で everybody will eat と everybody will be eaten と訳し分けられるように、敬語と動詞の受動態の二重の意味で使われます）。

　結局、賢治は猟師たちを「食べられないまま」にしておきます。賢治

の物語は、たいてい最後に道徳的な終わり方をします。復讐心で燃える
ような悲惨な終わり方をすることはめったにあまりありません。悪人や
不道徳な人物（この場合は猟師）を罰するのではなく、逃がすのです（し
かし、賢治の物語には例外がいくつかあります。そのひとつが『オツベ
ルと象』で、邪悪な資本家が悲惨な結末を迎えることになります）。

　賢治は、悪人が当然の報いを受け、私たちがそれを目撃して満足感を
得るということを許してはくれません。邪悪な者にも光が見えることを
教えてくれるのです。『ひかりの素足』では子どもたちを苦しめた残忍な
鬼たちは、仏陀と対面することで救いを見出します。

　『注文の多い料理店』には、猟師が窮地に陥るという愉快な物語を超
えた要素があります。この作品には、賢治が大人になってから追い求め
た理想の社会像にまつわるテーマが数多く含まれています。

　21歳のときに、賢治はベジタリアンになりました。現在、日本ではベ
ジタリアンやビーガンと呼ばれる人は人口の6％程度と言われています。
その数はフランスやアメリカの数とほぼ同じですが、オーストラリアや
北欧諸国の人口比での半分程度です。

　賢治が21歳になったのは、1917年です。当時、日本では動物の肉を
食べないという人は非常に少なく、肉を食べないのは、おそらくは精進
料理が出される寺の関係の人たちに限られていたと思われます。しかし、
賢治が住んでいた地方では、貧しい人たちは皿の上に干物が少しあるだ
けで感謝していたでしょうから、賢治が「野菜中心の食事にしなさい」
と言っても、当然、人々は動じることはありませんでした。

　賢治は、輪廻転生を信じていたので、人間は動物を殺してはならない

と考えていました。狩猟のテーマはいくつかの物語に登場します。『なめとこ山の熊』では、猟師が物語の中心の登場人物になっています。猟師になる選択肢しかない貧しい小十郎は、獲物と運命を共にすることになります。一方、『注文の多い料理店』では、猟師たちは紙一重のところで生き残ることができます。

　動物福祉は、世界中で大きな問題となっています。多くの国で動物の権利を守るための法律が制定され、動物が自然の摂理に従って自由に生きることができるようになりつつあります。現在の定義では人間だけの権利を示す「人権」という言葉が、すべての動物に適用される日が来てほしいものです。

　動物福祉をテーマにした賢治の作品の中で、最もドラマチックなのは『フランドン農学校の豚』です。これは畜殺されるために肥育される豚の悲劇を描いたものです。動物の権利に関して書かれた世界で最も早い物語のひとつでしょう。

　最後に、オノマトペをふんだんに使った賢治の最も有名な文のひとつが、『注文の多い料理店』に登場します。

> 　風がどうと吹いてきて、草はざわざわ、木の葉はかさかさ、木は
>
> ごとんごとんと鳴りました。

(p.61)

　これから始まる食欲をそそるごちそうに備える自然の声が聞こえてきそうですね。

Two young gentlemen, dressed in an utterly British military fashion with rifles sparkling on their shoulders and two dogs that resembled polar bears at their heels, were chatting to each other as they went on their way amidst the rustling leaves deep into the very heart of the mountains.

"Damn these mountains, that's what I say. No birds or animals here either. I'm just itching to blast something and I don't care what it is!"

"I'd get such a kick out of planting two or three shots smack between the yellow ribs of a deer. It'd spin round before hitting the dirt with the hugest thud!"

They were really in the heart of the mountains now, so deep that even their guide, a professional hunter, had lost his bearings and gone off somewhere.

What's more, the mountains were so scary that the two dogs resembling polar bears both became dizzy, growled for a while, frothed at the mouth and promptly died.

"Well, there goes 2,400 yen," said one of the gentlemen, briefly rolling back his dog's eyelid.

"I'm down 2,800, you know," said the other bitterly, his head drooping down.

The first gentleman, looking off color and disgruntled, studied the face of the second gentleman as he spoke.

"I reckon it's time to be heading back."

"You know, I've just been feeling rather cold and hungry, and I was thinking the very same thing."

"Well, then, let's call it a day. Come what may, we can buy ourselves about ten yen worth of wild fowl at yesterday's inn and take that home with us."

二人の若い紳士が、すっかりイギリスの兵隊のかたちをして、ぴかぴかする鉄砲をかついで、白熊のような犬を二疋つれて、だいぶ山奥の、木の葉のかさかさしたとこを、こんなことを言いながら、あるいておりました。

「ぜんたい、ここらの山は怪しからんね。鳥も獣も一疋も居やがらん。なんでも構わないから、早くタンタアーンと、やって見たいもんだなあ。」

「鹿の黄いろな横っ腹なんぞに、二三発お見舞もうしたら、ずいぶん痛快だろうねえ。くるくるまわって、それからどたっと倒れるだろうねえ。」

それはだいぶの山奥でした。案内してきた専門の鉄砲打ちも、ちょっとまごついて、どこかへ行ってしまったくらいの山奥でした。

それに、あんまり山が物凄いので、その白熊のような犬が、二疋いっしょにめまいを起して、しばらく吠って、それから泡を吐いて死んでしまいました。

「じつにぼくは、二千四百円の損害だ」と一人の紳士が、その犬の眼ぶたを、ちょっとかえしてみて言いました。

「ぼくは二千八百円の損害だ。」と、もひとりが、くやしそうに、あたまをまげて言いました。

はじめの紳士は、すこし顔いろを悪くして、じっと、もひとりの紳士の、顔つきを見ながら言いました。

「ぼくはもう戻ろうとおもう。」

「さあ、ぼくもちょうど寒くはなったし腹は空いてきたし戻ろうとおもう。」

「そいじゃ、これで切りあげよう。なあに戻りに、昨日の宿屋で、山鳥を拾円も買って帰ればいい。」

utterly 「すっかり」、まったく、完全に

at their heels すぐあとについて

itching to blast something 「早くタンタアーンと、やって見たいもんだなあ」(itching to...: すぐに〜したくてたまらない)

get such a kick out of... 「痛快」、〜を楽しむ、〜でスリルや快感を覚える

planting 打ち込む、埋め込む

hitting the dirt 「倒れる」、地面に伏せる

with the hugest thud 「どたっと」(thud: ドシンという音)

heart of the mountains 「山奥」

lost his bearings 「まごついて」、方向を見失った、道に迷った

growled 「吠って」

frothed at the mouth 「泡を吐いて」

off color 「顔いろを悪くして」

disgruntled 不満な、不機嫌な

let's call it a day 「切り上げよう」

wild fowl 「山鳥」、野鳥

"Saw some rabbits there too. No one'll know the difference. Okay, let's get going back."

However, the awful thing about it was that they didn't have the foggiest idea of which way back was.

The wind bellowed, the grass swished, the leaves rustled and the trees rumbled low.

"You know, I'm starving. My sides have been aching since way back there."

"Me too. I don't feel like taking another step. God, what can we do? I'd give my right eye for something to eat."

"I could eat a horse."

That's what the two gentlemen said as they made their way through the swishing pampas grass. Then suddenly they looked back to see a magnificent European-style house behind them. A sign on the front door said ...

"Hey, just what the doctor ordered. This place here is pretty civilized. Why don't we just go on in!"

"Gosh, who would've expected it in a place like this? Anyway, they're bound to be serving up something in there."

"Of course they're serving up something. Can't you read the sign?"

「兎もでていたねえ。そうすれば結局おんなじこった。では帰ろうじゃないか」

ところがどうも困ったことは、どっちへ行けば戻れるのか、いっこうに見当がつかなくなっていました。

風がどうと吹いてきて、草はざわざわ、木の葉はかさかさ、木はごとんごとんと鳴りました。

「どうも腹が空いた。さっきから横っ腹が痛くてたまらないんだ。」

「ぼくもそうだ。もうあんまりあるきたくないな。」

「あるきたくないよ。ああ困ったなあ、何かたべたいなあ。」

「喰べたいもんだなあ」

二人の紳士は、ざわざわ鳴るすすきの中で、こんなことを言いました。

その時ふとうしろを見ますと、立派な一軒の西洋造りの家がありました。

そして玄関には

> RESTAURANT
> 西洋料理店
> WILDCAT HOUSE
> 山 猫 軒

という札がでていました。

「君、ちょうどいい。ここはこれでなかなか開けてるんだ。入ろうじゃないか」

「おや、こんなとこにおかしいね。しかしとにかく何か食事ができるんだろう」

「もちろんできるさ。看板にそう書いてあるじゃないか」

うさぎ（兎）

bellowed 「どうと吹いて」、とどろいて、うなって

swished 「ざわざわ」、（風などが）シュっと鳴った

rustled 「かさかさ」、（葉などが）サラサラ鳴った

rumbled 「ごとんごとん」、ごろごろ鳴った、とどろいた

pampas grass 「すすき」

civilized 「開けてる」、文明化している

bound to be... ～にちがいない

"What're we waiting for, then? If I don't get some food into this belly of mine, I'll be a goner."

The two men stood in the entrance hall. It was a truly grand hall made of white porcelain bricks. This notice appeared in gilded lettering on the glass French doors in front of them.

> Feel Free To Enter Whoever You Are
> Please Do Make Yourselves At Home

The two men, beside themselves with joy, spoke up.

"Well, how do you like that, things are really coming our way here. We got ourselves into a pickle all day today, but we've made it now. This place is a restaurant, but they don't charge for their meals."

"Looks that way, doesn't it. That's what they mean when they say 'Please do make yourselves at home.' "

The two men pushed the doors open and entered, coming right into a corridor. This was written in gilded lettering on the inside of the glass doors ...

> We Particularly Welcome With Open Arms
> Plump And Young Individuals

The two men were overjoyed at being welcomed with open arms.

"See, we're being taken in with open arms."

"Because we're both plump and young, that's why."

They strode down the corridor to a door painted sky blue.

「はいろうじゃないか。ぼくはもう何か喰べたくて倒れそうなんだ。」

二人は玄関に立ちました。玄関は白い瀬戸の煉瓦で組んで、実に立派なもんです。

そして硝子の開き戸がたって、そこに金文字でこう書いてありました。

「どなたもどうかお入りください。決してご遠慮はありません」

二人はそこで、ひどくよろこんで言いました。

「こいつはどうだ、やっぱり世の中はうまくできてるねえ、きょう一日なんぎしたけれど、こんどはこんないいこともある。このうちは料理店だけれどもただでご馳走するんだぜ。」

「どうもそうらしい。決してご遠慮はありませんというのはその意味だ。」

二人は戸を押して、なかへ入りました。そこはすぐ廊下になっていました。その硝子戸の裏側には、金文字でこうなっていました。

「ことに肥ったお方や若いお方は、大歓迎いたします」

二人は大歓迎というので、もう大よろこびです。

「君、ぼくらは大歓迎にあたっているのだ。」

「ぼくらは両方兼ねてるから」

ずんずん廊下を進んで行きますと、こんどは水いろのペンキ塗りの扉がありました。

goner　助かる見込みのない者

gilded lettering　「金文字」

things are really coming our way　事がうまく運ぶ

got ourselves into a pickle　「なんぎした」、苦境に陥った

with open arms　心から、大いに

Plump　「肥った」、肉付きのよい

taken in　（人）を泊める、受け入れる。take in を受動態にすることで「だまされる」や「罠にかかる」という意味にもなるため、ここではこの先の2人の行方を暗示している

"This place is weird, you know. What're all these doors doing here?"

"It's the Russian style. It's always like this in cold places and in the mountains."

Then, as they went to open the door, they noticed some yellow writing above it.

> This Restaurant Is A Restaurant Of Many Orders
> We Beg Your Indulgence

"Must be doing a roaring business! Way out here, of all places."

"You bet. I mean, even your big Tokyo restaurants are mostly off the main streets, aren't they?"

The two men opened the door as they spoke. On the other side of it ...

> You May Find There Are Many Orders
> But Please Put Up With All Of Them

"What in the hell do they mean by that?" said one gentleman, scowling.

"Yeah, well, they must mean that they're apologizing for the delays because they've got their hands full due to the large number of orders."

"That must be it. I wish I could get right into one of the rooms, though."

"And I'm dying to sit myself down at a table."

「どうも変な家だ。どうしてこんなにたくさん戸があるのだろう。」

「これはロシア式だ。寒いとこや山の中はみんなこうさ。」

そして二人はその扉をあけようとしますと、上に黄いろな字でこう書いてありました。

> 「当軒は注文の多い料理店ですからどうかそこはご承知ください」

「なかなかはやってるんだ。こんな山の中で。」

「それあそうだ。見たまえ、東京の大きな料理屋だって大通りにはすくないだろう」

二人は言いながら、その扉をあけました。するとその裏側に、

> 「注文はずいぶん多いでしょうがどうか一々こらえて下さい。」

「これはぜんたいどういうんだ。」ひとりの紳士は顔をしかめました。

「うん、これはきっと注文があまり多くて支度が手間取るけれどもごめん下さいとこういうことだ。」

「そうだろう。早くどこか室の中にはいりたいもんだな。」

「そしてテーブルに座りたいもんだな。」

We Beg Your Indulgence 「ご承知ください」、ご辛抱ください

doing a roaring business 「はやってる」、大盛況である

Put Up With... 「こらえて」、我慢して

scowling 「顔をしかめ」

But unfortunately there was another door there to annoy them. There was also a mirror hanging beside it and, below the mirror, a brush with a long handle. The following words were written in red lettering on the door ...

> To Our Most Valued Customers
> Kindly Straighten Your Hair Here
> And Remove Mud From Footwear

"Stands to reason. I was wrong to write them off back there at the front door as just a place in the woods."

"They're strict on etiquette. I bet they get a lot of pretty important people here all the time."

At this the two men combed their hair and removed the mud from their boots. And then, what do you know ... no sooner had they replaced the brush on its shelf than it became all fuzzy and blurry, then vanished ... and a wind howled into the room.

The two men clung to each other in alarm, banged the door open and entered the next room. If they didn't get back to their old selves quickly by eating some warm food, who knows what could happen. Another bizarre sign greeted them on the other side of the door ...

> Be Sure To Leave Your Firearms And Bullets Here

They noticed a black stand directly to one side.

"Makes good sense. It's not proper to eat and carry a rifle at the same time."

"Wow, they really must get a lot of pretty important people here."

ところがどうもうるさいことは、また扉が一つありました。そしてそのわきに鏡がかかって、その下には長い柄のついたブラシが置いてあったのです。

扉には赤い字で、

「お客さまがた、ここで髪をきちんとして、それからはきものの泥を落してください。」

と書いてありました。

「これはどうも尤もだ。僕もさっき玄関で、山のなかだとおもって見くびったんだよ」

「作法の厳しい家だ。きっとよほど偉い人たちが、たびたび来るんだ。」

そこで二人は、きれいに髪をけずって、靴の泥を落しました。

そしたら、どうです。ブラシを板の上に置くや否や、そいつがぼうっとかすんで無くなって、風がどうっと室の中に入ってきました。

二人はびっくりして、互によりそって、扉をがたんと開けて、次の室へ入って行きました。早く何か暖いものでもたべて、元気をつけて置かないと、もう途方もないことになってしまうと、二人とも思ったのでした。

扉の内側に、また変なことが書いてありました。

「鉄砲と弾丸をここへ置いてください。」

見るとすぐ横に黒い台がありました。

「なるほど、鉄砲を持ってものを食うという法はない。」

「いや、よほど偉いひとが始終来ているんだ。」

Stands to reason
「尤もだ」、理にかなっている

write them off （だめだと）みなす、決めつける

etiquette 「作法」

all fuzzy and blurry
「ぼうっとかすんで」

vanished 「無くなって」

howled 「どうっと」、（風などが）ヒューヒューとうなる

clung to each other
「互によりそって」、ぴったりくっついて、密着して

get back to their old selves 「元気をつけて」、元の（何かが起こる前の）自分に戻って

bizarre 「変な」、奇妙な

Firearms 「鉄砲」

The two of them removed their rifles, undoing their belts, and put them on the stand. There was another door, a black one ...

> Please Remove Your Hats, Overcoats And Boots

"What do you think, should we take them off?"

"We've got no choice. Off they go. They really must be pretty important people, I mean, the people in there."

The two men hung their hats and overcoats on hooks, yanked off their boots and padded through the door. Written on the other side was ...

> Please Leave Here All Necktie Pins, Cufflinks
> Glasses, Wallets And Anything Made Of Metal
> Particularly Items With Sharp Points

An impressive safe, painted black and with its door ajar and a key in the lock, stood directly to one side of the door.

"Oh, I reckon they're using electricity for their dishes. Metallic things are dangerous. Pointy things are especially dangerous in that case."

"Must be the case. So I guess you pay the bill on your way out."

"Looks that way."

"Must be. Sure."

The two men took off their glasses, removed their cufflinks, put everything in the safe and locked the door. A little farther along there was another door with a glass jar in front of it. The following words were written on the door ...

二人は鉄砲をはずし、帯皮を解いて、それを台の上に置きました。

　また黒い扉がありました。

　　　「どうか帽子と外套（がいとう）と靴をおとり下さい。」

　「どうだ、とるか。」

　「仕方ない、とろう。たしかによっぽどえらいひとなんだ。奥に来ているのは」

　二人は帽子とオーバーコートを釘（くぎ）にかけ、靴をぬいでぺたぺたあるいて扉の中にはいりました。

　扉（と）の裏側には、

　　　「ネクタイピン、カフスボタン、眼鏡、財布、その他金物類、ことに尖（とが）ったものは、みんなここに置いてください」

と書いてありました。扉のすぐ横には黒塗りの立派な金庫も、ちゃんと口を開けて置いてありました。鍵（かぎ）まで添えてあったのです。

　「ははあ、何かの料理に電気をつかうと見えるね。金気（かなけ）のものはあぶない。ことに尖（とが）ったものはあぶないとこう言うんだろう。」

　「そうだろう。して見ると勘定は帰りにここで払うのだろうか。」

　「どうもそうらしい。」

　「そうだ。きっと。」

　二人はめがねをはずしたり、カフスボタンをとったり、みんな金庫の中に入れて、ぱちんと錠をかけました。

　すこし行きますとまた扉（と）があって、その前に硝子（がらす）の壺（つぼ）が一つありました。扉にはこう書いてありました。

yanked off 「ぬいで」、ぐいっと引っぱって脱いで

padded 「ぺたぺたあるいて」

Cufflinks 「カフスボタン」

impressive 「立派な」、印象的な

safe 「金庫」

ajar 「開けて」、少し開いて

glass jar 「硝子の壺」

> Please Cover Your Face And Limbs
> With Cream From The Jar

The jar definitely appeared to be full of cream made from milk.

"What do they want us to put cream on for?"

"Well, you see, it's freezing outside, right? And the room's so warm that your skin will get chapped, and they want to protect you from that. It really looks like they've got some pretty important people in there. It means that, for all we know, we might rub shoulders with aristocrats!"

They two of them rubbed cream over their faces, then over their hands and finally, taking off their socks, over their feet too. After that there was still some cream left, so they slipped some of it into their mouth while pretending to smear it on their face. Then they rushed to open the door and saw on the inside ...

> Did You Apply The Cream Thoroughly?
> Did You Rub It Over Your Ears Too?

... and they found a small jar of cream there as well.

"Oh, yeah, I didn't do my ears. Think of how chapped the skin on them could've gotten. The proprietors here don't leave a thing to chance, do they."

"Yeah, they're real sticklers for details, they are. Now, I'm starving, but this place is all just one corridor after another."

Just then they found themselves standing in front of yet another door ...

「壺のなかのクリームを顔や手足にすっかり塗っ
てください。」

みるとたしかに壺のなかのものは牛乳のクリームでし
た。

「クリームをぬれというのはどういうんだ。」

「これはね、外がひじょうに寒いだろう。室(へや)のなかが
あんまり暖いとひびがきれるから、その予防なんだ。ど
うも奥には、よほどえらいひとがきている。こんなとこ
で、案外ぼくらは、貴族とちかづきになるかも知れない
よ。」

二人は壺のクリームを、顔に塗って手に塗ってそれか
ら靴下(くつした)をぬいで足に塗りました。それでもまだ残ってい
ましたから、それは二人ともめいめいこっそり顔へ塗る
ふりをしながら喰べました。

それから大急ぎで扉をあけますと、その裏側には、

「クリームをよく塗りましたか、耳にもよく塗り
ましたか、」

と書いてあって、ちいさなクリームの壺がここにも置い
てありました。

「そうそう、ぼくは耳には塗らなかった。あぶなく耳
にひびを切らすとこだった。ここの主人はじつに用意周
到だね。」

「ああ、細かいとこまでよく気がつくよ。ところでぼ
くは早く何か喰べたいんだが、どうもこうどこまでも廊
下じゃ仕方ないね。」

するとすぐその前に次の戸がありました。

Limbs 「手足」

chapped 「ひびがきれ
る」、ひび割れた

for all we know 「案
外」、おそらく、もしかし
たら

rub shoulders with...
「～とちかづきになる」、(有
名人などと)付き合う

aristocrats 「貴族」

smear 「塗る」

proprietors 「主人」、
オーナー

don't leave a thing to
chance 「用意周到」、成
り行きにまかせない、偶然
に頼らない

sticklers for details
「細かいとこまでよく気が
つく」、細部にこだわる

> The Food Will Be Ready Very Soon Now
> It Won't Be Even A Bare 15 Minutes
> Until Everybody's Eaten
> Please Sprinkle The Perfume In The Bottle
> All Over Your Heads

There was a gilded bottle of perfume in front of the door. The two men splashed perfume from it all over their head. The perfume, however, had a distinct fragrance of vinegar.

"This perfume stinks of vinegar. What in the hell is going on here?"

"Must be some mistake. The maid caught a cold or something and put in the wrong stuff."

They opened the door and went in. These words were written in big lettering on the back of the door ...

> All Of These Many Orders Have No Doubt Annoyed You
> You Have Our Sympathy
> You Have Reached The End Now
> We Only Ask That You Rub Salt From The Pot
> Thoroughly Into Your Skin

Sure enough, a splendid blue porcelain salt pot stood before them, but this time the two men stared at each other aghast, their faces swimming in cream.

"I smell a rat here, you know."

"Yeah, something's fishy here."

"When they say there are lots of orders, they mean they're doing the ordering on us."

「料理はもうすぐできます。

　　十五分とお待たせはいたしません。

　　すぐたべられます。

　　早くあなたの頭に瓶の中の香水をよく振りかけ
　　てください。」

　そして戸の前には金ピカの香水の瓶が置いてありまし
た。

　二人はその香水を、頭へぱちゃぱちゃ振りかけました。

　ところがその香水は、どうも酢のような匂がするので
した。

　「この香水はへんに酢くさい。どうしたんだろう。」

　「まちがえたんだ。下女が風邪でも引いてまちがえて
入れたんだ。」

　二人は扉をあけて中にはいりました。

　扉の裏側には、大きな字でこう書いてありました。

　　「いろいろ注文が多くてうるさかったでしょう。
　　お気の毒でした。

　　もうこれだけです。どうかからだ中に、壺の中
　　の塩をたくさんよくもみ込んでください。」

　なるほど立派な青い瀬戸の塩壺は置いてありました
が、こんどというこんどは二人ともぎょっとしてお互に
クリームをたくさん塗った顔を見合せました。

　「どうもおかしいぜ。」

　「ぼくもおかしいとおもう。」

　「沢山の注文というのは、向うがこっちへ注文してる
んだよ。」

distinct　紛れもない、
はっきりとした

splendid　「立派な」

porcelain　「瀬戸の」、
磁器製の

aghast　「ぎょっとし
て」、愕然として

I smell a rat here　「ど
うもおかしい」、うさんく
さい

something's fishy
「おかしいと思う」、何かあ
やしい

"You see, the way I figure, this European restaurant is not a place where they feed their customers European food, it's a place where they make European food out of their customers to eat them. It's uh, I ... I ... mean ... it's ... it's us who's the ..."

He was shaking and quaking so much that the words wouldn't come out.

"You mean, it's ... it's ... us who's going to be ...? Yipes!"

He too was shivering so much that he couldn't get the rest of his words out either.

"Let's get out of ..."

One of the gentlemen, shaking like a leaf, tried to push the door behind him but, wouldn't you know it, it wouldn't budge an inch. There was one more door farther along with two large keyholes in it. On the door were carvings of a silver knife and fork ...

> We Appreciate The Pains You Have Taken
> The Preparations Have Been Completed Admirably
> Now It Is Time For You To Be Consumed

That was the handwriting on the door. To cap it off, two blue eyeballs were ogling them through the keyholes.

"Yipes!" said one gentleman, trembling.

"Cripes!" said the other, shivering.

The two of them began to bawl. Then they heard whispering coming from the door.

"Oh no, they've caught on. Looks like they won't rub the salt in."

「だからさ、西洋料理店というのは、ぼくの考えるところでは、西洋料理を、来た人にたべさせるのではなくて、来た人を西洋料理にして、食べてやる家とこういうことなんだ。これは、その、つ、つ、つ、つまり、ぼ、ぼ、ぼくらが……。」がたがたがたがた、ふるえだしてもうものが言えませんでした。

「その、ぼ、ぼくらが、……うわあ。」がたがたがたがたふるえだして、もうものが言えませんでした。

「遁げ……。」がたがたしながら一人の紳士はうしろの戸を押そうとしましたが、どうです、戸はもう一分も動きませんでした。

奥の方にはまだ一枚扉があって、大きなかぎ穴が二つつき、銀いろのホークとナイフの形が切りだしてあって、

「いや、わざわざご苦労です。

大へん結構にできました。

さあさあおなかにおはいりください。」

と書いてありました。おまけにかぎ穴からはきょろきょろ二つの青い眼玉がこっちをのぞいています。

「うわあ。」がたがたがたがた。

「うわあ。」がたがたがたがた。

ふたりは泣き出しました。

すると戸の中では、こそこそこんなことを言っています。

「だめだよ。もう気がついたよ。塩をもみこまないようだよ。」

Yipes 「うわあ」、わあ、ひゃあ

wouldn't you know it 「どうです」、案の定、やっぱり

wouldn't budge an inch 「一分も動きませんでした」

carvings 「切りだし」、彫刻、彫りもの

Admirably 「大へん結構に」、見事に、立派に

To cap it off 「おまけに」、きわめつけに

ogling 「きょろきょろ～のぞいています」、じろじろと見る、いやらしい目で見る

Cripes! 「うわあ」、きゃあ

bawl 「泣き出し」、大声で泣き

caught on 「気がついた」、理解した、悟った

"What do you expect, eh? The boss can't write worth beans. 'All of these many orders have no doubt annoyed you ... you have our sympathy' ... writing like that, how stupid can you get!"

"What's the difference? He doesn't even toss us a bone, whatever we do."

"You said it. And he'll blame us if these two guys don't come in here."

"Let's call out to them, okay? Hey, customers. Come in now. Come on, don't be shy. The plates have been washed and the greens have been rubbed thoroughly with salt. All that remains is to arrange you tastefully among the greens on a clean white plate. Do come on in."

"Yeah, come on. You're welcome. Maybe you don't fancy salad. In that case, we'll put the fire on now and deep fry you. Don't just stand there!"

The painful ache in the gentlemen's heart caused their faces to crumple like scraps of paper. Quivering and shivering, they stared at each other and silently sobbed.

Snickering and sniggering came from the door, along with another loud call.

"Come on in! Come on in! If you cry like that you'll just smear all that nice cream off. Yes, sir, immediately, sir. We will have them for you momentarily. Now, gentlemen, gentlemen, what are you waiting for?"

"Get yourselves in here now. The boss has already tucked in his napkin, he's got his knife poised and he's licking his chops in anticipation of his customers."

The two gentlemen just wept and wept and wept and wept. Just then, sounds came out of the blue from behind them.

「あたりまえさ。親分の書きようがまずいんだ。あすこへ、いろいろ注文が多くてうるさかったでしょう、お気の毒でしたなんて、間抜けたことを書いたもんだ。」

「どっちでもいいよ。どうせぼくらには、骨も分けて呉れやしないんだ。」

「それはそうだ。けれどももしここへあいつらがはいって来なかったら、それはぼくらの責任だぜ。」

「呼ぼうか、呼ぼう。おい、お客さん方、早くいらっしゃい。いらっしゃい。いらっしゃい。お皿も洗ってありますし、菜っ葉ももうよく塩でもんで置きました。あとはあなたがたと、菜っ葉をうまくとりあわせて、まっ白なお皿にのせる丈けです。はやくいらっしゃい。」

「へい、いらっしゃい、いらっしゃい。それともサラドはお嫌いですか。そんならこれから火を起してフライにしてあげましょうか。とにかくはやくいらっしゃい。」

二人はあんまり心を痛めたために、顔がまるでくしゃくしゃの紙屑のようになり、お互にその顔を見合せ、ぶるぶるふるえ、声もなく泣きました。

中ではふっふっとわらってまた叫んでいます。

「いらっしゃい、いらっしゃい。そんなに泣いては折角のクリームが流れるじゃありませんか。へい、ただいま。じきもってまいります。さあ、早くいらっしゃい。」

「早くいらっしゃい。親方がもうナフキンをかけて、ナイフをもって、舌なめずりして、お客さま方を待っていられます。」

二人は泣いて泣いて泣いて泣いて泣きました。

そのときうしろからいきなり、

The boss can't write worth beans 「親分の書きようがまずいんだ」、親分は文章が下手くそだ（worth beans:〔否定文で〕全くだめだ）

You said it. 「それはそうだ」、そのとおりだ

crumple 「くしゃくしゃの」

Quivering and shivering 「ぶるぶるふるえ」

silently sobbed 「声もなく泣きました」

Snickering and sniggering 「ふっふっとわらって」（snicker、snigger: 忍び笑いをする、クスクス笑う）

got... poised 〜の準備が整った

licking his chops 「舌なめずりして」

"Ruff. Ruff. Grrrr-ruff!"

The two dogs that resembled polar bears came crashing through the door and charging into the room. The eyeballs in the keyholes disappeared in a flash as the dogs circled the room for a time, snarling and growling, then, barking loudly again, suddenly threw themselves at the door.

The door crashed open and the dogs flew through it as if being swallowed up. Then the gentlemen heard a meowing, a grunting, a rumbling and finally a rustling in the pitch darkness beyond the door. The room vanished in a cloud of smoke, and the gentlemen were standing in the grass, shivering and quivering from the cold. One look and they saw their coats and boots and wallets and necktie pins hanging off branches or strewn by the roots of a tree.

The wind bellowed, the grass swished, the leaves rustled and the trees rumbled low.

The dogs returned, groaning and growling. Then there was hollering from behind.

"Gentlemen! Gentlemen!"

This suddenly brought them back to life.

"Hullo, hullo, we're over here! Come quick!" they screamed.

The professional hunter, wearing a reed hood, approached, rustling through the grass. The two gentlemen were finally able to breathe easily. They ate the dumplings the hunter had with him, spent about ten yen on wild fowl on their way and went on home to Tokyo.

Be that as it may, neither their return to Tokyo nor long soaks in hot baths could bring those faces, crumpled like scraps of paper, back to normal again.

「わん、わん、ぐゎあ。」という声がして、あの白熊のような犬が二疋、扉をつきやぶって室の中に飛び込んできました。鍵穴の眼玉はたちまちなくなり、犬どもはうううとうなってしばらく室の中をくるくる廻っていましたが、また一声

「わん。」と高く吠えて、いきなり次の扉に飛びつきました。戸はがたりとひらき、犬どもは吸い込まれるように飛んで行きました。

その扉の向うのまっくらやみのなかで、

「にゃあお。くゎあ、ごろごろ。」という声がして、それからがさがさ鳴りました。

室はけむりのように消え、二人は寒さにぶるぶるふるえて、草の中に立っていました。

見ると、上着や靴や財布やネクタイピンは、あっちの枝にぶらさがったり、こっちの根もとにちらばったりしています。風がどうと吹いてきて、草はざわざわ、木の葉はかさかさ、木はごとんごとんと鳴りました。

犬がふうとうなって戻ってきました。

そしてうしろからは、

「旦那あ、旦那あ、」と叫ぶものがあります。

二人は俄かに元気がついて

「おおい、おおい、ここだぞ、早く来い。」と叫びました。

簑帽子をかぶった専門の猟師が、草をざわざわ分けてやってきました。

そこで二人はやっと安心しました。

そして猟師のもってきた団子をたべ、途中で十円だけ山鳥を買って東京に帰りました。

しかし、さっき一ぺん紙くずのようになった二人の顔だけは、東京に帰っても、お湯にはいっても、もうもとのとおりになおりませんでした。

Ruff 「わん」
Grrrr-ruff! 「ぐゎあ」
snarling 「うなって」
strewn 「ちらばった」、まき散らされた
reed hood 「簑帽子」
long soaks in hot baths 「お湯にはいって」

グスコーブドリの伝記
The Life of Budory Goosko

イラスト：ルーシー・パルバース

The Life of Budory Goosko を読むまえに

真の自己犠牲の精神

幻想的な仕掛けの中に「賢治リアリズム」とも言える断片を仕込んだ作品。
寒冷化に直面したイーハトーブで、火山局の職員ブドリが下した決断とは。

　宮沢賢治の数ある作品の中でも『グスコーブドリの伝記』は、最も予言的な作品としての特徴を備えたものでしょう。

　この中編小説は、ブドリという青年が、両親と妹のネリとともに苦難にみちた人生を歩む物語です。両親は自暴自棄になって命を絶ち、妹のネリは謎の人物に誘拐され、まだ幼いブドリはひとりぼっちになってしまうという悲劇的な状況です。

　この作品はイーハトーブの地で、ブドリがさまざまな冒険をし、さまざまな人と出会っていく物語です。架空の地イーハトーブは、日本と同様に火山と地震の国でもあります。

　ブドリは、本物の鬼才であるクーボー大博士との出会いをきっかけに、天職である火山局への就職を果たし働くようになります。この火山局でブドリは、賢治が岩手県の農民のためにしたように、イーハトーブの農民の生活を向上させるために生涯を捧げることになるのです。

　『グスコーブドリの伝記』の文体や使われる言葉は一見幻想的に感じられますが、賢治は自分なりの「誇張されたリアリズム」の万華鏡の中に絶妙な断片を組み立てています。私は、宮沢賢治を「ファンタジー作家」と呼ぶことに異論を唱え、「賢治リアリズム」という造語を作りました。拙著『賢治から、あなたへ』（集英社インターナショナル）で指摘したように、彼の物語に登場する名前や事件のほとんどは、現実的な根拠を持つものです。『銀河鉄道の夜』の主人公ジョバンニの名前の由来も、ブドリの妹ネリの名前も、歴史上の実在の人物に由来しています。ジョバンニのモデルとなるのは、イタリアの有名な考古学者のジョバンニ・バティスタ・デ・ロッジ（1822-94）だと私は考えています。一方、ネリの名前は、貧者に生涯をささげた聖職者、フィリップ・ネリ（1515-95）から取られたものでしょう。賢治は、リアリティを再加工し、それを光と音の物

語に作り直すわけです。

『グスコーブドリの伝記』は、自然を破壊することなく、自然から直接得られるエネルギー源を探すこと、つまり、自然と調和してその力を利用することの必要性を説いた物語です。これだけで、この物語のテーマは21世紀に完全に通用するものになっています。

この作品が書かれた100年前（賢治は1922年に別のタイトルで書き始め、1931年に筆を擱いた）には、気候変動の危機は地球温暖化ではなく、地球冷却化だと考えられていました。そのため、農民の苦悩を解決するためにブドリがとった手段は、この物語に書かれたような温暖化を目指す路線になっています。しかし、私たちは視点を変えるだけで、「自分たちの生活と福祉に対しては自らが責任を持つ」というメッセージが、現代の私たちにも完全に通じることに気づくのです。

賢治の物語に登場する人たちがそれぞれの行為に対してもつ動機は、彼にとって非常に重要なものです。なぜなら、賢治自身、人を助けたい、自分を犠牲にしても善行を行いたいという内なる欲求に突き動かされていたからです。『グスコーブドリの伝記』の終わり近く、賢治はブドリの自己犠牲の動機について洞察を与えています。

「ところが六月もはじめになって、まだ黄いろなオリザの苗や、芽を出さない樹を見ますと、ブドリはもう居ても立ってもいられませんでした。このままで過ぎるなら、森にも野原にも、ちょうどあの年のブドリの家族のようになる人がたくさんできるのです。」（*p.167*）

もし私たちが人生の中で何らかの困窮に陥ったり悲しみを経験したならば、その感情や知性を他人を助けることに向けなければならないと、賢治は語っているのです。賢治自身は、父親が事業で成功し、恵まれた

生活を送っていたにもかかわらず、恵まれない人々に共感する能力と深い思いやりの心をもっていました。だからこそ、東日本大震災の後、賢治の物語や詩は多くの人々に感動とインスピレーションを与えたのです。

「居ても立ってもいられません」という表現には、多くの英訳が可能で、not being able to contain oneself「自分を抑えることができない」、can't stand idly by「傍観することができない」、to be itching to do something「何かをしたくてうずうずしている」などと英訳することができます。私が選んだのは、Budory wasn't about to take the situation lying down.「この状況を甘んじて受けようとはしなかった」です。彼は自分が置かれている状況を変えるために、どっしり構えて、自らがどうするかを選ばなければならなかったのです。

ブドリは農民たちから意識を失うまで殴られ、踏みにじられてしまいます。そのことによって、ブドリは空から肥料が降ってくるような素晴らしい成果を火山局の仕事で出しても、農民の中には彼に共感をしない人たちがいることがわかるのです。革命的な思想や行動は、往々にして無知な反応を招くということを、賢治はブドリと農民の関係を通して教えてくれているのです。

人々の生活を向上させるために究極の犠牲を払う前に、ブドリは賢治を代弁するように次のように言いました。

「私のようなものは、これから沢山できます。私よりもっともっと何でもできる人が、私よりもっと立派にもっと美しく、仕事をしたり笑ったりして行くのですから。」(*p.*169)

ここで言われている人とは、今、ここにいる私たちに他なりません。

THE FOREST

Budory Goosko was born in the huge forests of Ihatov. His father, Nadory Goosko, was a renowned woodcutter who could cut down the tallest tree without a fuss, as if lulling a baby to sleep.

Budory had a younger sister called Neri. They played in the woods every day. They went far into the woods but never so far that they couldn't hear the rasp of their father's saw as he cut down his trees. The two of them picked raspberries there, rinsing them in a spring, and took turns imitating the cry of the turtledove, gazing all the while up at the sky. At these times, the birds sleepily returned their calls in one soft cry after another.

While their mother sowed the little field in front of their house with barley, the two of them spread a straw mat on the ground, sat down on it and simmered the leaves of orchids in a tin can. Before they knew it, all kinds of birds were flapping by over the crackly hair of their head, as if greeting them hello.

When it came time for Budory to go to school, the forest turned into a frightfully lonely place in the middle of the day. But then, later in the afternoon, Budory and Neri would go all around the forest writing the names of the trees on their trunks in red clay or half-burnt pieces of old charcoal, singing at the top of their voice.

They wrote, too, on a birch tree where hop vines growing from both sides of the path formed a trellis ...

To All Cuckoos Keep Out!

一、 森

　グスコーブドリは、イーハトーブの大きな森のなかに生まれました。お父さんは、グスコーナドリという名高い木樵りで、どんな巨きな木でも、まるで赤ん坊を寝かしつけるように訳なく伐ってしまう人でした。

　ブドリにはネリという妹があって、二人は毎日森で遊びました。ごしっごしっとおとうさんの樹を鋸く音が、やっと聴えるくらいな遠くへも行きました。二人はそこで木苺の実をとって湧水に漬けたり、空を向いてかわるがわる山鳩の啼くまねをしたりしました。するとあちらでもこちらでも、ぽう、ぽう、と鳥が睡そうに鳴き出すのでした。

　お母さんが、家の前の小さな畑に麦を播いているときは、二人はみちにむしろをしいて座って、ブリキ缶で蘭の花を煮たりしました。するとこんどは、もういろいろの鳥が、二人のぱさぱさした頭の上を、まるで挨拶するように啼きながらざあざあざあざあ通りすぎるのでした。

　ブドリが学校へ行くようになりますと、森はひるの間大へんさびしくなりました。そのかわりひるすぎには、ブドリはネリといっしょに、森じゅうの樹の幹に、赤い粘土や消し炭で、樹の名を書いてあるいたり、高く歌ったりしました。

　ホップの蔓が、両方からのびて、門のようになっている白樺の樹には、

　「カッコウドリ、トオルベカラズ」と書いたりもしました。

Ihatov 「イーハトーブ」。この物語の舞台となっている架空の町

renowned woodcutter 「名高い木樵り」

without a fuss 「訳なく」、大騒ぎせずに（fuss: 騒ぎ）

lulling a baby to sleep 「赤ん坊を寝かしつける」（lull：～をなだめる）

turtledove 「山鳩」

birch tree 「白樺の樹」

trellis （蔓をはわせる）格子棚

And so, Budory turned ten and Neri, seven. But, for some reason or other, the sun that year became strangely pale from springtime, and the pure white flowers of the magnolia trees just didn't blossom with the thawing of the snow, and even May saw days when sheets of sleety rain fell, and when July came it didn't bring so much as a day of heat, and the barley that was sown the year before had all white ears without grain and the flowers of most of the fruit trees just bloomed and fell straight to the ground.

Finally, fall arrived, but the chestnuts, too, were simply shells, and the oryza that they all ate every day, so vital to them, was all husk and no grain. There had never been a worse time for the fields.

Budory's father and mother spent a lot of time lugging firewood to the plains, and, with the winter they carried big logs to town on a sledge, but they lost heart every time, bringing back only meager amounts of flour to eat. Even so, they managed to get through the winter, and when spring came, they sowed the seeds that they had stored so carefully. But that year proved to be a repeat of the year before, and the fall brought with it a real famine. Not a single child could be found in school. Budory's father and mother both stopped doing any work, and there were times when, after what looked like grave deliberations, they took turns going to town, sometimes bringing back a few handfuls of millet and other times returning empty handed and at a total loss. The Gooskos passed the winter eating things like beechnuts, arrowroot, bracken stalks and the soft bark of trees.

The following spring saw both parents come down with some kind of horrible disease.

そして、ブドリは十になり、ネリは七つになりました。ところがどういうわけですか、その年は、お日さまが春から変に白くて、いつもなら雪がとけると間もなく、まっしろな花をつけるこぶしの樹もまるで咲かず、五月になってもたびたび霙がぐしゃぐしゃ降り、七月の末になっても一向に暑さが来ないために、去年播いた麦も粒の入らない白い穂しかできず、大抵の果物も、花が咲いただけで落ちてしまったのでした。

そしてとうとう秋になりましたが、やっぱり栗の木は青いからのいがばかりでしたし、みんなでふだんたべるいちばんたいせつなオリザという穀物も、一つぶもできませんでした。野原ではもうひどいさわぎになってしまいました。

ブドリのお父さんもお母さんも、たびたび薪を野原の方へ持って行ったり、冬になってからは何べんも巨きな樹を町へそりで運んだりしたのでしたが、いつもがっかりしたようにして、わずかの麦の粉などもって帰ってくるのでした。それでもどうにかその冬は過ぎて次の春になり、畑にはたいせつにしまって置いた種子も播かれましたが、その年もまたすっかり前の年の通りでした。そして秋になると、とうとうほんとうの饑饉になってしまいました。もうそのころは学校へ来るこどももまるでありませんでした。ブドリのお父さんもお母さんも、すっかり仕事をやめていました。そしてたびたび心配そうに相談しては、かわるがわる町へ出て行って、やっとすこしばかりの黍の粒など持って帰ることもあれば、なんにも持たずに顔いろを悪くして帰ってくることもありました。そしてみんなは、こならの実や、葛やわらびの根や、木の柔らかな皮やいろんなものをたべて、その冬をすごしました。けれども春が来たころは、お父さんもお母さんも、何かひどい病気のようでした。

thawing of the snow
「雪がとける」

sheets of sleety rain
「霙がぐしゃぐしゃ」、みぞれ混じりの大雨

white ears without grain 「粒の入らない白い穂」（ears：穂、grain：粒）

oryza 「オリザ」、イネ、米

husk （穀物などの）殻

lugging 重いものを持って行ったり、引きずったり

lost heart 「がっかりしたようにして」

famine 「饑饉」

deliberations 「相談」、討議

millet 「黍」

One day, Budory's father just sat there with his head gripped in his hands, plunged deep into thought.

"I'm just going to make a visit to the woods," he said, rising abruptly.

He hobbled out of the house and did not return, though the day had turned to pitch-black night. Budory and Neri both asked their mother what happened to their father, but all their mother did was stare in silence into their face.

On the evening of the next day, when the forest was enveloped in darkness, Budory and Neri's mother bolted up without warning, fed a heap of woodchips to the hearth, lighting up the entire house, told the two of them that she was going out to look for their father and that they should little by little eat the flour and things in the cupboard, and, like their father, staggered out of the house. Budory and Neri both cried and followed her, but she turned back to them and said in a scolding voice ...

"What disobedient children you are!"

She then walked briskly, tripping as she went, until she disappeared into the woods. Budory and Neri just paced back and forth and round and round, crying all the while. Finally, when they could stand it no longer, they, too, entered the forest, and, wandering and circling about by the hop plant trellis and the spring, they called out to their mother throughout the night. The stars twinkled among the trees as if trying to tell them something, and the birds shot through the darkness as if alarmed ... but no human voice was heard wherever they went. Finally, Budory and Neri returned to their house in a daze of exhaustion and were soon lost to sleep, dead to the world.

ある日お父さんは、じっと頭をかかえて、いつまでも
いつまでも考えていましたが、俄かに起きあがって、

「おれは森へ行って遊んでくるぞ」と言いながら、よろ
よろ家を出て行きましたが、まっくらになっても帰って
来ませんでした。二人がお母さんに、お父さんはどうし
たろうときいても、お母さんはだまって二人の顔を見て
いるばかりでした。

次の日の晩方になって、森がもう黒く見えるころ、お
母さんは俄かに立って、炉に榾をたくさんくべて家じゅ
うすっかり明るくしました。それから、わたしはお父さ
んをさがしに行くから、お前たちはうちに居てあの戸棚
にある粉を二人ですこしずつたべなさいと言って、やっ
ぱりよろよろ家を出て行きました。二人が泣いてあとか
ら追って行きますと、お母さんはふり向いて、

「何たらいうことをきかないこどもらだ。」と叱るよう
に言いました。そしてまるで足早に、つまずきながら森
へ入ってしまいました。二人は何べんも行ったり来たり
して、そこらを泣いて廻りました。とうとうこらえ切れ
なくなって、まっくらな森の中へ入って、いつかのホッ
プの門のあたりや、湧水のあるあたりをあちこちうろう
ろ歩きながら、お母さんを一晩呼びました。森の樹の間
からは、星がちらちら何か言うようにひかり、鳥はたび
たびおどろいたように暗の中を飛びましたけれども、ど
こからも人の声はしませんでした。とうとう二人はぼん
やり家へ帰って中へはいりますと、まるで死んだように
睡ってしまいました。

with his head
gripped in his hands
「頭をかかえて」

plunged deep into
thought 「いつまでも
考えていました」、深く考
え込んでいた（plunge
into…：どっぷりつかる）

disobedient 「いうこと
をきかない」、従順でない

hop plant trellis 「ホッ
プの門」、ホップをはわせ
た格子棚（trellis：格子）

in a daze of exhaustion
（疲れたために）「ぼんやり」
して

dead to the world
「死んだように睡って」

It was past noon the next day when Budory awoke.

He remembered what his mother had said about the food in the cupboard and, opening it, found a big bag with buckwheat flour and lots of beechnuts in it. Budory shook Neri awake, and they both moistened up some flour and lit a fire in the hearth just like when their parents were there.

After twenty days' time had slipped by, they heard someone at the door say, "Hello, anyone there?" Budory leapt to his feet, thinking that his father had come back, but standing outside the door was a man with a big basket on his back and a cutting look in his eye. The man produced a round rice cake from his basket.

"I'm here to help with the famine in these parts," he said, tossing them the rice cake. "Dig into this, kids."

Budory and Neri were staggered.

"Go on, eat. Eat it!" said the man.

Budory and Neri, unsure at first, took a few bites.

"You're good kids," said the man, peering into their eyes. "But it's not goin' to do you any good just bein' good kids. You should come along with me. But you, boy, are strong an' I can't take the two of you. But hey, little girl, there's nothin' for you to eat if you stay on here. Come with me to town, eh? I'll give you bread every day."

At that, the man lifted Neri straight up off the ground, shoved her right into the basket on his back, barked out, "Oh, goody goody, oh, goody goody," roared with laughter and flew out the door like the wind. Once outside, Neri began to weep and wail, as Budory dashed after them, crying and screaming, "Robber! Thief!" But the man had already passed along the edge of the forest and was flying through the distant meadow. All Budory could hear was the faint weeping and wailing of his sister Neri.

ブドリが眼をさましたのは、その日のひるすぎでした。お母さんの言った粉のことを思いだして戸棚を開けて見ますと、なかには、袋に入れたそば粉やこならの実がまだたくさん入っていました。ブドリはネリをゆり起して二人でその粉をなめ、お父さんたちがいたときのように炉に火をたきました。

それから、二十日ばかりぼんやり過ぎましたら、ある日戸口で、

「今日は、誰か居るかね。」と言うものがありました。お父さんが帰って来たのかと思ってブドリがはね出して見ますと、それは籠をしょった目の鋭い男でした。その男は籠の中から円い餅をとり出してぽんと投げながら言いました。

「私はこの地方の飢饉を救けに来たものだ。さあ何でも喰べなさい。」二人はしばらく呆れていましたら、

「さあ喰べるんだ、食べるんだ。」とまた言いました。二人がこわごわたべはじめますと、男はじっと見ていましたが、

「お前たちはいい子供だ。けれどもいい子供だというだけでは何にもならん。わしと一緒についておいで。尤も男の子は強いし、わしも二人はつれて行けない。おい女の子、おまえはここにいてももうたべるものがないんだ。おじさんと一緒に町へ行こう。毎日パンを食べさしてやるよ。」そしてぷいっとネリを抱きあげて、せなかの籠へ入れて、そのまま、「おおほいほい。おおほいほい。」とどなりながら、風のように家を出て行きました。ネリはおもてではじめてわっと泣き出し、ブドリは、「どろぼう、どろぼう。」と泣きながら叫んで追いかけましたが、男はもう森の横を通ってずうっと向うの草原を走っていて、そこからネリの泣き声が、かすかにふるえて聞えるだけでした。

buckwheat flour 「そば粉」

beechnuts 「こならの実」、ブナの実

cutting look in his eye 「目の鋭い」、鋭い目つき

rice cake 「餅」

staggered 「呆れて」、圧倒されて、呆然とさせられて

peer into their eyes 「じっと見て」、じっと目を見つめる

Budory followed them as far as the edge of the forest, sobbing and shouting, but soon he was completely out of breath and collapsed in a heap on the ground.

THE SILKWORM FACTORY

Budory abruptly opened his eyes and heard a flat, low-pitched voice coming from right over his head.

"So, you finally managed to wake up. Plannin' on starvin' to death, are ya? Well, get up and give me a hand."

A man with a brown mushroom of a cap on his head and an overcoat hugging his shirt was dangling something made of wire in front of him.

"Is the famine over?" asked Budory. "What am I supposed to give you a hand with?"

"Net throwing."

"Are you going to throw nets over here?"

"Yep, sure am."

"What are you going to do with them after that?"

"Breed silkworms, that's what."

Two men on ladders seemed to be hard at work casting nets over the chestnut trees, adjusting them here and there. Yet the nets were so fine that Budory couldn't see their threads.

"Is that how you raise silkworms?"

ブドリは、泣いてどなって森のはずれまで追いかけて行きましたが、とうとう疲れてばったり倒れてしまいました。

二、 てぐす工場

ブドリがふっと眼をひらいたとき、いきなり頭の上で、いやに平べったい声がしました。

「やっと眼がさめたな。まだお前は飢饉（きゝん）のつもりかい。起きておれに手伝わないか。」

見るとそれは茶いろなきのこしゃっぽをかぶって外套（がいとう）にすぐシャツを着た男で、何か針金でこさえたものをぶらぶら持っているのでした。

「もう飢饉は過ぎたの？　手伝いって何を手伝うの？」ブドリがききました。

「網掛けさ。」

「ここへ網を掛けるの？」

「掛けるのさ。」

「網をかけて何にするの？」

「てぐすを飼うのさ。」

見るとすぐブドリの前の栗（くり）の木に、二人の男がはしごをかけてのぼっていて一生けん命何か網を投げたり、それを操ったりしているようでしたが、網も糸も一向見えませんでした。

「あれでてぐすが飼えるの？」

give me a hand 「おれに手伝わないか」

dangling 「ぶらぶら持っている」、ぶら下げている

net throwing 「網掛け」

breed silkworms 「てぐすを飼う」、蚕を飼う

"Yep, sure is. You're a persistent little kid, you know that? Listen here, you're starting this off on the wrong foot, little man. It takes more than luck to get something like this off the ground. Why would I go puttin' up a silkworm factory in a place where ya couldn't produce thread? We're all set up to do it here. There's actually a lot of folks like me makin' ends meet out here doin' this very thing."

"Oh, well then …" Budory finally eked out in a scratchy voice.

"An' besides, seein' as I've bought up all the woodland here, you can work here if you want or, if not, you can just get lost and go off somewhere else. I mean, it's not as if you're goin' to find anything more to eat anywhere else, is it."

"If that's the case, I'll help out," said Budory, barely managing to hold back his tears. "But, why are you casting nets over the trees?"

"Sure, look, I'll tell you all about it. See this?" With both his hands the man pulled on the wires of what looked like a cage. "See? If you pull like this, you get yourself a ladder."

The man strode over to the chestnut tree on his right and hooked the wire ladder onto a low branch.

"Now, try and take this net up to the top. Go on, climb up now."

The man handed Budory a funny-looking ball-like object. There was nothing for Budory to do but take it and, holding fast to the ladder, he started to climb up. The rungs of the wire ladder were thin and they virtually bit into his hands and feet.

"Keep climbin'! Higher, higher! Now, throw that ball I gave you. Throw it right over the chestnut tree. Throw it high up into the sky. What's the matter with you, shakin' like a leaf? Good-for-nothin' kid! Throw it. Throw the damn thing, will ya!"

「飼えるのさ。うるさいこどもだな。おい。縁起でもないぞ。てぐすも飼えないところにどうして工場なんか建てるんだ。飼えるともさ。現におれはじめ沢山のものが、それでくらしを立てているんだ。」

ブドリはかすれた声で、やっと、「そうですか。」と言いました。

「それにこの森は、すっかりおれが買ってあるんだから、ここで手伝うならいいが、そうでもなければどこかへ行って貰いたいな。もっともお前はどこへ行ったって食うものもなかろうぜ。」

ブドリは泣き出しそうになりましたが、やっとこらえて言いました。

「そんなら手伝うよ。けれどもどうして網をかけるの？」

「それは勿論教えてやる。こいつをね。」男は手にもった針金の籠のようなものを両手で引き伸ばしました。「いいか。こういう工合にやるとはしごになるんだ。」

男は大股に右手の栗の木に歩いて行って、下の枝に引っ掛けました。

「さあ、今度はおまえが、この網をもって上へのぼって行くんだ。さあ、のぼってごらん。」

男は変なまりのようなものをブドリに渡しました。ブドリは仕方なくそれをもってはしごにとりついて登って行きましたが、はしごの段々がまるで細くて手や足に喰いこんでちぎれてしまいそうでした。

「もっと登るんだ。もっと、もっとさ。そしたらさっきのまりを投げてごらん。栗の木を越すようにさ。そいつを空へ投げるんだよ。何だい。ふるえてるのかい。意気地なしだなあ。投げるんだよ。投げるんだよ。そら、投げるんだよ。」

Budory had no choice but to fling the ball-like object with all his might up into the blue sky. But just then the sun shone black in his eyes and he fell topsy-turvy out of the tree toward the ground. The man caught him, lifted him away from the ladder and absolutely flipped his lid.

"You're really good for nothin', aren't ya! What a little namby-pamby you are! If I hadn't caught you just now, you would've split your noggin right open. You owe me your life, little man, and I won't tolerate your insolence from now on. Now, get over to that tree and get yourself up it and I'll give you somethin' to eat in a bit."

The man handed Budory another ball. Budory carried the ladder to the next tree and flung the ball over its branches.

"Thataboy, I think you've got the hang of it. Now, I've got a lot of balls where that one came from, so stay on the ball. Any one of these chestnut trees will do."

The man took some ten balls from his pockets, gave them to Budory and marched off. But, casting just three of them made Budory short of breath and completely worn out, and he hobbled over to the house that was his home. But now, to his utter surprise, the house had a chimney made of red earthenware pipes sticking out of its roof, and over the front door a sign that read ...

THE IHATOV SILKWORM FACTORY

The man from before came out of the house smoking a pipe.

"Well, kid, I've got somethin' for you to eat here. Fill your belly and then get on the job again while it's still light."

"I won't do it. I'm going home."

ブドリは仕方なく力一杯にそれを青空に投げたと思いましたら俄かにお日さまがまっ黒に見えて逆さまに下へ落ちました。そしていつか、その男に受けとめられていたのでした。男はブドリを地面におろしながらぷりぷり憤り出しました。

　「お前もいくじのないやつだ。何というふにゃふにゃだ。俺が受け止めてやらなかったらお前は今ごろは頭がはじけていたろう。おれはお前の命の恩人だぞ。これからは、失礼なことを言ってはならん。ところで、さあ、こんどはあっちの木へ登れ。も少したったらごはんもたべさせてやるよ。」男はまたブドリへ新しいまりを渡しました。ブドリははしごをもって次の樹へ行ってまりを投げました。

　「よし、なかなか上手になった。さあまりは沢山あるぞ。なまけるな。樹も栗の木ならどれでもいいんだ。」

　男はポケットから、まりを十ばかり出してブドリに渡すと、すたすた向うへ行ってしまいました。ブドリはまた三つばかりそれを投げましたが、どうしても息がはあはあしてからだがだるくてたまらなくなりました。もう家へ帰ろうと思って、そっちへ行って見ますと愕いたことには、家にはいつか赤い土管の煙突がついて、戸口には「イーハトーブてぐす工場」という看板がかかっているのでした。そして中からたばこをふかしながら、さっきの男が出て来ました。

　「さあこども、たべものをもってきてやったぞ。これを食べて暗くならないうちにもう少し稼ぐんだ。」

　「ぼくはもういやだよ。うちへ帰るよ。」

the sun shone black in his eyes 「お日さまがまっ黒に見えて」

fell topsy-turvy out of the tree 「逆まに下へ落ちました」（topsy-turvy：逆さまに）

flipped his lid 「憤り出しました」。これはイディオム（flip：正気を失う、かっとなる）

namby-pamby 「いくじのない」、気弱な

noggin 「頭」

insolence 「失礼なこと」、無礼な言動

"Home? You mean this place? This place isn't your home anymore, kid. It's my factory. The house and all the woodland here, I bought it an' it's all mine now."

Budory was so desperate that he took the steamed bun the man was holding out and, without saying a word, marched over to a tree to cast another ten balls of net over its branches.

That night, Budory curled up into a little ball and fell asleep in the corner of what used to be his home but was now a silkworm factory.

The factory owner sat by the fire till late, drinking and talking with a few men that Budory didn't recognize. At the crack of dawn, Budory went into the woods and worked as he had the day before.

When about a month had gone by and all the chestnut trees in the forest were covered in nets, the factory owner had his men hang five or six rough planks of wood in the branches of every tree. Each plank was covered in what looked like grains of millet. Before long, the trees were sprouting leaves and the whole forest had turned an ashen blue. After a while, countless little pale-white worms were crawling off the boards and up onto the branches of the trees, leaving trails of thread behind them.

Budory and the other workers were now put to work gathering firewood every day and piling it up at the sides of the house. Pale white strings of flowers were blossoming throughout the branches of the chestnut trees, and the worms that had crawled in the branches blended in perfectly with them. After that, all the leaves on all the chestnut trees were eaten away until not even a trace of them was left.

Before long the worms were spinning large yellow cocoons throughout the mesh of the nets.

「うちっていうのはあすこか。あすこはおまえのうちじゃない。おれのてぐす工場だよ。あの家もこの辺の森もみんなおれが買ってあるんだからな。」

ブドリはもうやけになって、だまってその男のよこした蒸しパンをむしゃむしゃたべて、またまりを十ばかり投げました。

その晩ブドリは、昔のじぶんのうち、いまはてぐす工場になっている建物の隅に、小さくなってねむりました。さっきの男は、三、四人の知らない人たちと遅くまで炉ばたで火をたいて、何か呑んだりしゃべったりして居ました。次の朝早くから、ブドリは森に出て、昨日のようにはたらきました。

それから一月ばかりたって、森じゅうの栗の木に網がかかってしまいますと、てぐす飼いの男は、こんどは栗のようなものがいっぱいついた板きれを、どの木にも五六枚ずつ吊させました。そのうちに木は芽を出して森はまっ青になりました。すると、木につるした板きれから、たくさんの小さな青じろい虫が、糸をつたわって列になって枝へ這いあがって行きました。ブドリたちはこんどは毎日薪とりをさせられました。その薪が、家のまわりに小山のように積み重なり、栗の木が青じろい紐のかたちの花を枝いちめんにつけるころになりますと、あの板から這いあがって行った虫も、ちょうど栗の花のような色とかたちになりました。そして森じゅうの栗の葉は、まるで形もなくその虫に食い荒らされてしまいました。それから間もなく虫は、大きな黄いろな繭を、網の目ごとにかけはじめました。

woodland 「森」

desperate 「やけになって」

steamed bun 「蒸しパン」

marched over to... 〜のところにさっさと行った

curled up into a little ball and fell asleep 「小さく（丸く）なってねむりました」

crack of dawn 「朝早く」、夜明け

planks of wood 「板きれ」

what looked like grains of millet 「栗のようなもの」(millet：キビ、アワ・ヒエ)

sprouting leaves 「芽を出して」

ashen blue 「まっ青」、青白い（ashen：灰のような、）

pale-white worms 「青じろい虫」

Pale white strings of flowers 「青じろい紐のかたちの花」

cocoons 「繭」

That was when the silkworm factory owner went positively berserk, hollering at Budory and the others to rush about and collect cocoons into baskets. He had cocoons put into cauldrons and boiled up furiously, after which the gathered thread was spun on three spinning wheels that rattled away day and night. When half the little house was full of yellow spun thread, huge white moths began to flip and flap out of the cocoons that had been left outside, flitting into the air. The factory owner, his face lit up like a demon's, now began to gather up the thread himself, and he brought four more men from the fields to join him in the work. The number of moths leaving their cocoons had grown with the days, and, in the end, it was as if snow itself was fluttering throughout the forest. Then, one day, several horse-drawn carts arrived and were loaded up with the entire store of thread before starting back toward town, followed by the workers. When the very last cart was about to leave, the silkworm factory owner turned to Budory.

"Hey, I've left enough food in the house to last you till spring. You stay here and guard the forest and the factory, you hear?"

And having said that, he followed the last cart away with a weird smirk on his face.

するとてぐす飼いの男は、狂気のようになって、ブドリたちを叱りとばして、その繭を籠に集めさせました。それをこんどは片っぱしから鍋に入れてぐらぐら煮て、手で車をまわしながら糸をとりました。夜も昼もがらがらがらがら三つの糸車をまわして糸をとりました。こうしてこしらえた黄いろな糸が小屋に半分ばかりたまったころ、外に置いた繭からは、大きな白い蛾がぽろぽろぽろぽろ飛びだしはじめました。てぐす飼いの男は、まるで鬼みたいな顔つきになって、じぶんも一生けん命糸をとりましたし、野原の方からも四人人を連れてきて働かせました。けれども蛾の方は日ましに多く出るようになって、しまいには森じゅうまるで雪でも飛んでいるようになりました。するとある日、六七台の荷馬車が来て、いままでにできた糸をみんなつけて、町の方へ帰りはじめました。みんなも一人ずつ荷馬車について行きました。いちばんしまいの荷馬車がたつとき、てぐす飼いの男が、ブドリに、

「おい、お前の来春まで食うくらいのものは家の中に置いてやるからな、それまでここで森と工場の番をしているんだぞ。」

と言って変ににやにやしながら、荷馬車についてさっさと行ってしまいました。

positively berserk
（本当に）「狂気のようになって」

hollering 「叱り飛ばして」、大声で言って

cauldrons 「鍋」、大釜

yellow spun thread
「黄いろな糸」

moths 「蛾」

flip and flap out of...
「〜からぽろぽろぽろぽろ飛びだし」（flip：ぴくぴくと動く、flap：パタパタと動く）

with a weird smirk
「変ににやにやしながら」

Budory was left alone in a daze. The inside of the house was a filthy mess, as if ravaged by a storm, and the woods themselves had been laid waste to, as if a wildfire had swept right through them. When, the next day, Budory started to clean up the house and the area around it, he came across an old cardboard box where the silkworm factory owner had often sat. There were some ten books crammed into the box. He opened the books and saw many pictures of silkworms and drawings of machines. There were also books that went above his head and those that contained pictures of various trees and plants with their names written under them.

Budory spent that winter diligently copying down the words and the drawings that were in the books.

When spring came, the factory owner appeared again, this time most impeccably dressed, bringing with him a number of new hands. From the next day, they all began to work exactly as they had the year before.

All the nets were cast over the trees and the yellow boards hung from the branches. The worms crawled off the boards up onto the branches. Budory and the others were set to work gathering firewood. One morning, when they were piling up the firewood, the earth began to shudder and quake. Then, far in the distance, a tremendous boom was heard.

After a while the day turned bizarrely dark, a fine ash came fluttering down, and a pure white sheet blanketed the forest. Budory and the others crouched down in shock under the trees, and the factory owner scurried over in a huff.

ブドリはぼんやりあとへ残りました。うちの中はまるで汚くて、嵐のあとのようでしたし森は荒れはてて山火事にでもあったようでした。ブドリが次の日、家のなかやまわりを片附けはじめましたらてぐす飼いの男がいつも座っていた所から古いボール紙の函を見附けました。中には十冊ばかりの本がぎっしり入って居りました。開いて見ると、てぐすの絵や機械の図がたくさんある、まるで読めない本もありましたし、いろいろな樹や草の図と名前の書いてあるものもありました。

ブドリは一生けん命その本のまねをして字を書いたり図をうつしたりしてその冬を暮しました。

春になりますとまたあの男が六、七人のあたらしい手下を連れて、大へん立派ななりをしてやって来ました。そして次の日からすっかり去年のような仕事がはじまりました。

そして網はみんなかかり、黄いろな板もつるされ、虫は枝に這い上り、ブドリたちはまた、薪作りにかかるころになりました。ある朝、ブドリたちが薪をつくっていましたら俄かにぐらぐらっと地震がはじまりました。それからずうっと遠くでどーんという音がしました。

しばらくたつと日が変にくらくなり、こまかな灰がばさばさばさばさ降って来て、森はいちめんにまっ白になりました。ブドリたちが呆れて樹の下にしゃがんでいましたら、てぐす飼いの男が大へんあわててやってきました。

laid waste to 「荒れはてて」

went above his head 「まるで読めない」、理解を超えた

diligently 「一生けん命」

impeccably dressed 「大へん立派ななりをして」、一分の隙もない服装をして

quake 「地震」

tremendous boom 「どーんという音」、（地震などが）とどろく大きな音

scurried over in a huff 「大へんあわててやってきた」

"Hey, all of you, it's over. It's an eruption. The thing has started to erupt. The silkworms have all been covered in ash and are dead. Everyone pull out. Hey, Budory, you can stick around if you want, but there won't be any food left for you this time. Besides, it's dangerous to stay on. You're better off getting yourself to the fields and working there, do you hear?"

No sooner had he said that than he was scurrying away and gone. Budory went to the factory to have a look there, but the place was deserted. So, downhearted and dejected, he headed for the plain, stepping into the footsteps that had been left by the others in the white ash.

THE MARSH PADDIES

Budory continued to walk for half a day through the ash-covered woods toward town. Every time a wind blew, ash fluttered down from the trees in a blizzard of smoke. The closer he got to the plain, the thinner and sparser the cover of ash became, until once again the trees looked green and footsteps vanished in the sloshy road.

「おい、みんな、もうだめだぞ。噴火だ。噴火がはじまったんだ。てぐすはみんな灰をかぶって死んでしまった。みんな早く引き揚げてくれ。おい、ブドリ。お前ここに居たかったら居てもいいが、こんどはたべ物は置いてやらないぞ。それにここに居ても危いからなお前も野原へ出て何か稼ぐ方がいいぜ。」そう言ったかと思うと、もうどんどん走って行ってしまいました。ブドリが工場へ行って見たときはもう誰も居りませんでした。そこでブドリは、しょんぼりとみんなの足痕のついた白い灰をふんで野原の方へ出て行きました。

三、 沼ばたけ

　ブドリは、いっぱいに灰をかぶった森の間を、町の方へ半日歩きつづけました。灰は風の吹くたびに樹からばさばさ落ちて、まるでけむりか吹雪のようでした。けれどもそれは野原へ近づくほど、だんだん浅く少くなって、ついには樹も緑に見え、みちの足痕も見えないくらいになりました。

eruption 「噴火」
THE MARSH
PADDIES 「沼ばたけ」
(marsh：沼、paddy：
水田)
sloshy road　ぬかるんだ道

When he finally made his way out of the woods, Budory found himself gazing ahead in astonishment. Before his eyes, all the way to the clouds in the distance white as snow, paddies lay before him like so many beautifully pink, green and gray cards. As he approached them, he saw that the pink came from a low blanket of flowers and that honeybees were busy going from one to another, that the green was from densely growing grasses on which little ears had formed, and that the gray came off the shallow mud of the marsh. All of these had been marked off by low narrow embankments, and people were using horses to dig up and plough the paddies.

Budory walked among the paddies for a time. Two men were having what sounded like a fierce argument in the middle of the road. The man on the right, sporting a red beard, said to the other man, who was old and tall and wearing a white rush hat ...

"I'm a man who bets and runs risks in whatever I do."

The other man then said ...

"When I said give it up, I meant it! You can pile on as much manure as you like, but all you're goin' to get is straw without a single grain."

"Humph, the way I estimate it, it's going to be three times hotter this summer than up to now, take my word for it. I'm going to take in three years' worth of grain in one year."

"Give it up while you're ahead, I say. Forget it."

"Humph, there's no way in the world I'd do that. I've already composted heaps of flowers and beans and enough chicken manure for a hundred thousand square meters. We don't have all day here and I need all the help I can get. That's why I've come to you."

Budory, in spite of himself, went up to the men and bowed.

とうとう森を出切ったとき、ブドリは思わず眼をみはりました。野原の眼の前から、遠くのまっしろな雲まで、美しい桃いろと緑と灰いろのカードでできているようでした。そばへ寄って見ると、その桃いろなのには、いちめんにせいの低い花が咲いていて、蜜蜂がいそがしく花から花をわたってあるいていましたし、緑いろなのには小さな穂を出して草がぎっしり生え、灰いろなのは浅い泥の沼でした。そしてどれも、低い幅のせまい土手でくぎられ、人は馬を使ってそれを掘り起したり掻き廻したりしてはたらいていました。

ブドリがその間を、しばらく歩いて行きますと、道のまん中に、二人の人が、大声で何か喧嘩でもするように言い合っていました。右側の方の鬚の赭い人が言いました。

「何でもかんでも、おれは山師張るときめた。」

するともう一人の白い笠をかぶったせいの高いおじいさんがいいました。

「やめろって言ったらやめるもんだ。そんなに肥料うんと入れて、藁はとれるっったって、実は一粒もとれるもんでない。」

「うんにゃ、おれの見込みでは、今年は今までの三年分暑いに相違ない。一年で三年分とって見せる。」

「やめろ。やめろ。やめろったら。」

「うんにゃ。やめない。花はみんな埋めてしまったから、こんどは豆玉を六十枚入れてそれから鶏の糞、百駄入れるんだ。急がしったら何のこう忙しくなれば、ささげの蔓でもいいから手伝いに頼みたいもんだ。」

ブドリは思わず近寄っておじぎをしました。

little ears had formed
「小さな穂を出して」

embankments 「土手」

dig up and plough
「堀り起したり掻き廻したり」、掘り起こしたり耕したり

sporting a red beard
「鬚の赭い（ひげのあかい）」、これ見よがしに赤いひげを生やしている

white rush hat 「白い笠」、白いイグサの笠
（rush：ここではイグサ）

bets and runs risks
「山師張る」、山をかける

all you're goin' to get is straw without a single grain 「藁（わら）はとれるっったって、実は一粒もとれるもんでない」、藁は取れるが実は一粒もとれない

Give it up while you're ahead. いいかげんにやめて。give it up のかわりに quit も使える。これは決まり文句

chicken manure 「鶏の糞」

in spite of himself
「思わず」、われ知らず

"Well, then, how about using me?" he said.

At that the two men, looking most startled, put their hands to their chin and stared at Budory. The man with the red beard suddenly burst out laughing.

"Sure, sure. You can hold the horse's bit. Follow me right now. So, it's put up or shut up. Just you watch me till the fall. Well, let's go. All I wanted was a little help when I needed it," said the man with the red beard now to Budory, now to the other man, as he walked away from them both.

"You'll be weepin' into your whiskers for not listenin' to what an old man has to say to ya," muttered the other man as he watched the man with the red beard walk away, followed by Budory.

Each day Budory used a horse to turn the muddy soil. Each day saw the pink and green gradually squashed down into a bog. From time to time the horse kicked up muddy water that splashed into everyone's face. When one paddy was done, he took the horse into the next one. Each day was very long, and, in the end, he didn't know if he was standing or walking, and the mud just looked to him like squishy candy or watery soup. The wind barely stopped howling, forming ripples like fish scales on the muddy water nearby and turning the water in the distance the color of tin. Bittersweet clouds puffed through the sky every day as slow as blazes, and Budory looked up at them with an envious eye.

「そんならぼくを使ってくれませんか。」

　すると二人は、ぎょっとしたように顔をあげて、あごに手をあててしばらくブドリを見ていましたが、赤鬚が俄かに笑い出しました。

　「よしよし。お前に馬の指竿とりを頼むからな。すぐおれについて行くんだ。それではまず、のるかそるか、秋まで見ててくれ。さあ行こう。ほんとに、ささげの蔓でもいいから頼みたい時でな。」赤鬚は、ブドリとおじいさんに交る交る言いながら、さっさと先に立って歩きました。あとではおじいさんが、

　「年寄りの言うこと聞かないで、いまに泣くんだな。」とつぶやきながら、しばらくこっちを見送っているようすでした。

　それからブドリは、毎日毎日沼ばたけへ入って馬を使って泥を掻き廻しました。一日ごとに桃いろのカードも緑のカードもだんだん潰されて、泥沼に変るのでした。馬はたびたびぴしゃっと泥水をはねあげて、みんなの顔へ打ちつけました。一つの沼ばたけがすめばすぐ次の沼ばたけへ入るのでした。一日がとても永くて、しまいには歩いているのかどうかわからなくなったり、泥が飴のような、水がスープのような気がしたりするのでした。風が何べんも吹いて来て近くの泥水に魚の鱗のような波をたて、遠くの水をブリキいろにして行きました。そらでは、毎日甘くすっぱいような雲が、ゆっくりゆっくりながれていて、それがじつにうらやましそうに見えました。

hold the horse's bit
「馬の指竿（させ）とり」
をする

put up or shut up
「のるかそるか」、我慢して
やるか黙るか

squashed down into
a bog　「だんだん潰され
て、泥沼に変るのでした」
（bog：沼）

forming ripples like
fish scales　「魚の鱗の
ような波をたて」

Some twenty days passed like that until all of the paddies were, at last, soft mud. The next morning, the owner of the fields, all worked up, joined all of the people who had gathered from here, there and everywhere, to plant oryza seedlings, like little green lances, in every bit of paddy mud. That took some ten days, and when it was done, he took Budory and the others to work at the houses of people who had helped out in the paddies. And when that work was finished, he returned to his own paddies and weeded and weeded and weeded some more. The owner's oryza plants grew so thick they looked black, while the neighboring paddies were a fuzzy light green, making it easy to see the border between the two from far away. After seven days of weeding, they all went away again to help others in their work.

But, one morning, when the owner was taking Budory around his paddies, he suddenly stood bolt upright and screamed, "Ah!" Even his lips had turned pale blue as he stood erect, gazing vacantly over his paddies.

"It's definitely a disease," he finally said.

"Do you have a headache," asked Budory.

"Not me, the oryza! That!"

The owner pointed to the stalks of the oryza in front of them. Budory crouched down to get a better look, seeing that it was true. All of the leaves were speckled with red dots the likes of which he had never seen before. The owner plodded with a heavy heart once around his paddies, then started off for home. Budory followed. He was terribly worried about him. At home, the owner wet a cloth, wrung it out, put it on his head and fell asleep right there on the wooden floor. It was then that his wife came running in from outside.

こうして二十日ばかりたちますと、やっと沼ばたけはすっかりどろどろになりました。次の朝から主人はまるで気が立って、あちこちから集まって来た人たちといっしょに、その沼ばたけに緑いろの槍のようなオリザの苗をいちめん植えました。それが十日ばかりで済むと、今度はブドリたちを連れて、今まで手伝って貰った人たちの家へ毎日働きにでかけました。それもやっと一まわり済むと、こんどはまたじぶんの沼ばたけへ戻って来て、毎日毎日草取りをはじめました。ブドリの主人の苗は大きくなってまるで黒いくらいなのに、となりの沼ばたけはぼんやりしたうすい緑いろでしたから、遠くから見ても、二人の沼ばたけははっきり堺まで見わかりました。七日ばかりで草取りが済むとまたほかへ手伝いに行きました。ところがある朝、主人はブドリを連れて、じぶんの沼ばたけを通りながら、俄かに「あっ」と叫んで棒立ちになってしまいました。見ると唇のいろまで水いろになって、ぼんやりまっすぐを見つめているのです。

　「病気が出たんだ。」主人がやっと言いました。

　「頭でも痛いんですか。」ブドリはききました。

　「おれでないよ。オリザよ。それ。」主人は前のオリザの株を指さしました。ブドリはしゃがんでしらべて見ますと、なるほどどの葉にも、いままで見たことのない赤い点々がついていました。主人はだまってしおしおと沼ばたけを一まわりしましたが、家へ帰りはじめました。ブドリも心配してついて行きますと、主人はだまって巾を水でしぼって、頭にのせると、そのまま板の間に寝てしまいました。すると間もなく、主人のおかみさんが表からかけ込んで来ました。

lances 「槍」

stood bolt upright
「棒立ちになって」

plodded... once
around 「しおしおと
〜を一まわりしました」
（plod：とぼとぼと歩く）

"Is it true that the oryza's diseased?"

"Yeah, it's all finished."

"Isn't there anything you can do?"

"Don't think so. It's just like what happened five years ago."

"That's why I told you to give up being a speculator, didn't I? Grandpa did his best to try to stop you, too."

She looked completely rattled and burst into tears. At that, her husband abruptly sat up.

"Got it," he said, suddenly in good spirits. "Am I not one of the greatest farmers these fields of Ihatov have ever seen ... am I going to let a little thing like this defeat me? Got it! Next year I'm going to beat this thing. Budory, you've not really slept a single night since you first came to my home, have you. Well, you sleep as long as you like, five days, ten days, however many days. After that, you're going to see the amazing tricks I can conjure up in those marsh paddies. But because of what happened, we'll all be eating only buckwheat this winter. You like buckwheat, I'm sure."

Having said that, the owner of the paddies hurriedly donned his hat and left.

Budory did as the owner said and went to the stables to sleep. But the marsh paddies were weighing on his mind, and he made his way over there with leaden feet. The owner, too, had gone there. He was standing all alone on an embankment with his arms folded over his chest. The paddies were full of water, the oryza stalks had barely given off leaves, and petrol was gleaming off the surface of the water.

"I'm now in the process of choking off this disease."

「オリザへ病気が出たというのはほんとうかい。」

「ああ、もうだめだよ。」

「どうにかならないのかい。」

「だめだろう。すっかり五年前の通りだ。」

「だから、あたしはあんたに山師をやめろといったんじゃないか。おじいさんもあんなにとめたんじゃないか。」おかみさんはおろおろ泣きはじめました。すると主人が俄かに元気になってむっくり起きあがりました。

「よし。イーハトーブの野原で、指折り数えられる大百姓のおれが、こんなことで参るか。よし。来年こそやるぞ。ブドリ。おまえおれのうちへ来てから、まだ一晩も寝たいくらい寝たことがないな。さあ、五日でも十日でもいいから、ぐうというくらい寝てしまえ。おれはそのあとで、あすこの沼ばたけでおもしろい手品をやって見せるからな。その代り今年の冬は、家じゅうそばばかり食うんだぞ。おまえそばはすきだろうが。」それから主人はさっさと帽子をかぶって外へ出て行ってしまいました。ブドリは主人に言われた通り納屋へ入って睡ろうと思いましたが、何だかやっぱり沼ばたけが苦になって仕方ないので、またのろのろそっちへ行って見ました。するといつ来ていたのか、主人がたった一人腕組みをして土手に立って居りました。見ると沼ばたけには水がいっぱいで、オリザの株は葉をやっと出しているだけ、上にはぎらぎら石油が浮んでいるのでした。主人が言いました。

「いまおれこの病気を蒸し殺してみるとこだ。」

speculator 「山師」、投機家、相場師

rattled 「おろおろ」、困惑した

conjure up 「手品をやって見せる」、呪文で呼び出す

petrol 「石油」

"Will the petrol kill off what's causing the disease?" asked Budory.

"I've doused the place in petrol, and even a human would die from that," said the owner, taking a deep breath and shrugging a shoulder.

Just then the owner of the neighboring paddies down from his approached.

"What are you doin' puttin' petrol in the water?" he yelled, stiffening his shoulders and out of breath. "It's all run down my way."

"What do you mean what am I doin'?" answered the owner, cool as a cucumber. "When oryza gets diseased, you put petrol in the water."

"Yeah, you do that and it all runs down to me."

"Well, what do you expect it to do? Water flows down, so naturally the petrol is goin' to flow with it."

"So, if that's naturally what's goin' to happen, why didn't you block up the place where it flows through, eh?"

"You wanna know why I didn't block off the place where the water flows down your way? It's because that part of the paddy isn't mine so I can't go blockin' it off, that's why!"

The other man was so furious he couldn't speak, so instead, he all of a sudden splashed right into the water of one of his paddies and began to block off the opening with handfuls of mud.

"He's a tough nut," said the owner, grinning. "If I blocked off the opening on my side, he'd still blow his stack and blame me, so I've got him to do it on his side. All he has to do is block it off in one place there and my paddies will fill up with water to the tops of the plants in a single night. Now, let's go."

The owner started off at a brisk pace toward home.

「石油で病気の種が死ぬんですか。」とブドリがききますと、主人は、

「頭から石油に漬けられたら人だって死ぬだ。」と言いながら、ほうと息を吸って首をちぢめました。その時、水下の沼ばたけの持ち主が、肩をいからして息を切ってかけて来て、大きな声でどなりました。

「何だって油など水へ入れるんだ、みんな流れて来て、おれの方へはいってるぞ。」

主人は、やけくそに落ちついて答えました。

「何だって油など水へ入れるったって、オリザへ病気がついたから、油など水へ入れるのだ。」

「何だってそんならおれの方へ流すんだ。」

「何だってそんならおまえの方へ流すったって、水は流れるから油もついて流れるのだ。」

「そんなら何だっておれの方へ水来ないように水口とめないんだ。」

「何だっておまえの方へ水行かないように水口とめないかったって、あすこはおれのみな口でないから水とめないのだ。」

となりの男は、かんかん怒ってしまってもう物も言えず、いきなりがぶがぶ水へはいって、自分の水口に泥を積みあげはじめました。主人はにやりと笑いました。

「あの男むずかしい男でな。こっちで水をとめると、とめたといって怒るからわざと向うにとめさせたのだ。あすこさえとめれば、今夜中に水はすっかり草の頭までかかるからな。さあ帰ろう。」主人はさきに立ってすたすた家へあるきはじめました。

cool as a cucumber
「やけくそに落ちついて」、
落ち着きはらって

tough nut 「むずかしい
男」、扱いにくい人

blow his stack 「怒
る」、カッとなる

The next morning, Budory went back to the marsh paddies with the owner, who picked a single leaf from the water and examined it thoroughly, pulling a long face. The same thing happened the day after that, too. And the day after that. And the day after that. On the morning after that, the owner finally said determinedly …

"So, Budory, it's high time we started sowing buckwheat. Go on over there and break down that barrier to the other paddies."

Budory did what the owner said and broke down the barrier. Water with petrol in it flowed into the neighboring paddies with a frightening force. They were sure that the owner of those paddies would blow his stack again, and, sure enough, at just about noon, he did come back, this time wielding an enormous sickle.

"What in the hell do you think you're doin', releasing petrol into my paddies?!"

"What's wrong with a bit of petrol once in a while?" said the owner in his usual calm low voice.

"It'll kill off all of my oryza."

"Kill it off or not, just have a look at the oryza in my paddies, will ya? This is the fourth day since I covered the plants with petrol. And, you can see for yourself what the result is. The ones with the red spots are the sick ones, the vigorous ones are that way because of the petrol. The petrol has only barely flowed up to the stalks in your paddy. Might do 'em the world of good, for all I know."

次の朝ブドリはまた主人と沼ばたけへ行ってみました。主人は水の中から葉を一枚とってしきりにしらべていましたが、やっぱり浮かない顔でした。その次の日もそうでした。その次の日もそうでした。その次の日もそうでした。その次の朝、とうとう主人は決心したように言いました。

　「さあブドリ、いよいよここへ蕎麦播きだぞ。おまえあすこへ行って、となりの水口こわして来い。」ブドリは、言われた通りこわして来ました。石油のはいった水は、恐ろしい勢でとなりの田へ流れて行きます。きっとまた怒ってくるなと思っていますと、ひるごろ例のとなりの持ち主が、大きな鎌をもってやってきました。

　「やあ、何だってひとの田へ石油ながすんだ。」

　主人がまた、腹の底から声を出して答えました。

　「石油ながれれば何だって悪いんだ。」

　「オリザみんな死ぬでないか。」

　「オリザみんな死ぬか、オリザみんな死なないか、まずおれの沼ばたけのオリザ見なよ。きょうで四日頭から石油かぶせたんだ。それでもちゃんとこの通りでないか。赤くなったのは病気のためで、勢のいいのは石油のためなんだ。おまえの所など、石油がただオリザの足を通るだけでないか。却っていいかもしれないんだ。」

pulling a long face
「浮かない顔」をして

wielding an enormous sickle 「大きな鎌をもって」、大きな鎌を振り回して（wield：振り回す、sickle：鎌）

"You mean, the petrol's a kind of manure?" said the other owner, now not looking as angry as before.

"Don't ask me whether it'll act as a manure or not. All I know is that petrol's an oil."

"Yep, it's an oil, all right," said the man, now in a much better mood.

The water level was quite low now, and the oryza stalks were exposed right down to the roots, covered in red blotches that resembled burns.

"Well, I'm goin' to cut down all my plants now anyway," said the owner with a laugh.

He and Budory then cut down every single plant at the stalk, sowed buckwheat, covered the seeds with earth and left. And just as the owner had predicted, Budory spent the entire winter eating only buckwheat. When spring came, the owner said to him ...

"Budory, the number of working paddies is down this year a third compared to last year, so the work won't be nearly as tiring. So, in place of the work, I want you to study hard the books that my son who died read and figure out ways to produce a great crop of oryza that'll amaze all those people who laughed at me and called me a speculator."

At that, he gave Budory a huge stack of all sorts of books. Budory went through them one after the other when he had time off work. The most interesting of those books were the ones with the ideas and thoughts of a man named Koobow. Budory read those books over and over and desperately wanted to go to Ihatov City so that he could study at the school where Prof. Koobow taught a month-long course.

「石油こやしになるのか。」向うの男は少し顔いろをやわらげました。

「石油こやしになるか石油こやしにならないか知らないが、とにかく石油は油でないか。」

「それは石油は油だな。」男はすっかり機嫌を直してわらいました。水はどんどん退き、オリザの株は見る見る根もとまで出て来ました。すっかり赤い斑ができて焼けたようになっています。

「さあおれの所ではもうオリザ刈りをやるぞ。」

主人は笑いながら言って、それからブドリといっしょに、片っぱしからオリザの株を刈り、跡へすぐ蕎麦を播いて土をかけて歩きました。そしてその年はほんとうに主人の言ったとおり、ブドリの家では蕎麦ばかり食べました。次の春になりますと主人が言いました。

「ブドリ、今年は沼ばたけは去年よりは三分の一減ったからな、仕事はよほど楽だ。その代りおまえは、おれの死んだ息子の読んだ本をこれから一生けん命勉強して、いままでおれを山師だといってわらったやつらを、あっと言わせるような立派なオリザを作る工夫をして呉れ。」そして、いろいろな本を一山ブドリに渡しました。ブドリは仕事のひまに片っぱしからそれを読みました。殊にその中の、クーボーという人の物の考え方を教えた本は面白かったので何べんも読みました。またその人が、イーハトーブの市で一ケ月の学校をやっているのを知って、大へん行って習いたいと思ったりしました。

red blotches 「赤い斑」
（blotch：しみ、できもの）
stalk 「株」、根、茎
Koobow 「クーボー」。
主人公があとで訪ねていく
学者の名前

By the time the summer had rolled well along, Budory had distinguished himself admirably in his work for the marsh paddy owner. He stopped the disease from attacking the oryza plants as it had the year before by using wood ash and salt. By mid-August, all of the stalks were boasting fine ears, and on each and every ear a little white flower blossomed, flowers that gradually produced pale-blue grains, all of which swayed in waves with the wind. The owner, full of pride, felt triumphant.

"What do ya say?" he boasted to whoever showed up. "I bungled the crop for four years speculating on oryza, but this year I'm takin' in four years' worth. That's about as good as it gets, wouldn't you say?"

But the year after that did not go as well. It didn't rain at all from the time of planting, the paddies dried out, cracks formed in the mud, and the fall harvest proved barely sufficient to provide food for the winter. The owner was counting on the year after that, but the drought that year was just as bad as the previous year. Every year he counted on the next, as, little by little, he was able to afford less and less manure, sold off his horse and, eventually, let go of most of the paddies, too.

そして早くもその夏、ブドリは大きな手柄をたてました。それは去年と同じ頃、またオリザに病気ができかかったのを、ブドリが木の灰と食塩を使って食いとめたのでした。そして八月のなかばになると、オリザの株はみんなそろって穂を出し、その穂の一枝ごとに小さな白い花が咲き、花はだんだん水いろの籾にかわって、風にゆらゆら波をたてるようになりました。主人はもう得意の絶頂でした。来る人ごとに、

「何のおれも、オリザの山師で四年しくじったけれども、今年は一度に四年前とれる。これもまたなかなかいいもんだ。」などと言って自慢するのでした。

ところがその次の年はそうは行きませんでした。植え付けの頃からさっぱり雨が降らなかったために、水路は乾いてしまい、沼にはひびが入って、秋のとりいれはやっと冬じゅう食べるくらいでした。来年こそと思っていましたが次の年もまた同じようなひでりでした。それからも来年こそ来年こそと思いながら、ブドリの主人は、だんだんこやしを入れることができなくなり、馬も売り、沼ばたけもだんだん売ってしまったのでした。

By the time the summer had rolled well along 「早くもその夏」、夏が十分進むまでには

distinguished himself admirably in his work 「大きな手柄をたてました」（distinguish oneself：名を上げる、admirably：立派に、みごとに）

wood ash 「木の灰」

swayed in waves with the wind 「風にゆらゆら波をたてるようになりました」

bungled 「しくじった」

was counting on the year after that 「来年こそと思っていました」、翌年に期待して（count on...：〜を当てにする、〜に期待する）

One fall day, the owner bitterly told Budory ...

"Budory, I used to be a great farmer here in Ihatov and once made myself piles of money, but because of the cold and the drought that keep coming, I own only one-third of the paddies I once did, and I haven't got any more manure left for next year. It's not only me. There's almost no one left in Ihatov who can buy manure to use. This being so, I don't know when I'd be able to pay you for the work you would do for me. I'd hate to see you wasting your best years living with me like this. I'm really sorry, but take this and go where you can to find good fortune."

Having said that, the owner gave Budory a bag of money, a suit of clothes made of hemp dyed navy blue and a pair of red leather shoes.

Budory forgot all about how hard the work there had been and thought that he didn't need anything at all and that he just wanted to keep working. But then he realized that there wouldn't be much work for him to do if he stayed on, so he thanked the owner profusely, parted with the man and the paddies he had known for six years and started off in the direction of the station.

ある秋の日、主人はブドリにつらそうに言いました。
　「ブドリ、おれももとはイーハトーブの大百姓だった
し、ずいぶん稼いでも来たのだが、たびたびの寒さと
旱魃のために、いまでは沼ばたけも昔の三分の一になっ
てしまったし、来年は、もう入れるこやしもないのだ。
おれだけでない。来年こやしを買って入れれる人ったら
もうイーハトーブにも何人もないだろう。こういうあん
ばいでは、いつになっておまえにはたらいて貰った礼を
するというあてもない。おまえも若いはたらき盛りを、
おれのとこで暮してしまってはあんまり気の毒だから、
済まないがどうかこれを持って、どこへでも行っていい
運を見つけてくれ。」そして主人は一ふくろのお金と新ら
しい紺で染めた麻の服と赤革の靴とをブドリにくれまし
た。ブドリはいままでの仕事のひどかったことも忘れて
しまって、もう何にもいらないから、ここで働いていた
いとも思いましたが、考えてみると、居てもやっぱり仕
事もそんなにないので、主人に何べんも何べんも礼を言っ
て、六年の間はたらいた沼ばたけと主人に別れて停車場
をさして歩きだしました。

hemp 「麻」
profusely 「何べんも何
べんも」、過度に

THE GREAT PROFESSOR KOOBOW

Budory walked for about two hours until he came to the station. Then he bought a ticket and boarded the train for Ihatov City. The train went ahead at full speed, rapidly leaving behind one marsh paddy after another; and the dense black woods beyond them seemed to change their shape as they receded into the distance. Budory's heart was full of many thoughts and feelings. He wanted to get to Ihatov City as soon as he could and meet the man called Koobow who had written those heart-warming books, and, if possible, study there while working out a way to compensate for things like volcanic ash and drought and cold summers, so that all the people would be able to harvest their crop without suffering and worry ... and thinking all this made the train seem like it was just crawling along.

The train arrived at Ihatov City in the afternoon of that day. He stepped off it and lingered for a while, listening to the bubbling sounds coming up from the ground and staring at the overcast sky and standing in a daze amid the many cars that were racing by him. He snapped out of that daze and asked people there how to get to Prof. Koobow's school. All the people he asked simply burst out laughing at the sight of Budory's earnest face.

"Never heard of a school like that," they said.

"Just keep walkin' another five or six blocks and ask someone again," they said.

It was nearly evening by the time Budory found the school. Someone was speaking in a loud voice on the second floor of that big crumbling white building.

四、 クーボー大博士

　ブドリは二時間ばかり歩いて、停車場へ来ました。それから切符を買って、イーハトーブ行きの汽車に乗りました。汽車はいくつもの沼ばたけをどんどんどんどんうしろへ送りながら、もう一散に走りました。その向うには、たくさんの黒い森が、次から次と形を変えて、やっぱりうしろの方へ残されて行くのでした。ブドリはいろいろな思いで胸がいっぱいでした。早くイーハトーブの市に着いて、あの親切な本を書いたクーボーという人に会い、できるなら、働きながら勉強して、みんながあんなにつらい思いをしないで沼ばたけを作れるよう、また火山の灰だのひでりだの寒さだのを除く工夫をしたいと思うと、汽車さえまどろこくってたまらないくらいでした。汽車はその日のひるすぎ、イーハトーブの市に着きました。停車場を一足出ますと、地面の底から何かのんのん湧くようなひびきやどんよりとしたくらい空気、行ったり来たりする沢山の自働車のあいだに、ブドリはしばらくぼうとしてつっ立ってしまいました。やっと気をとりなおして、そこらの人にクーボー博士の学校へ行くみちをたずねました。すると誰へ訊いても、みんなブドリのあまりまじめな顔を見て、吹き出しそうにしながら、「そんな学校は知らんね。」とか、「もう五六丁行って訊いて見な。」とかいうのでした。そしてブドリがやっと学校をさがしあてたのはもう夕方近くでした。その大きなこわれかかった白い建物の二階で、誰か大きな声でしゃべっていました。

receded into the distance 「うしろの方へ残されて行くのでした」、次第に遠ざかっていった

overcast sky 「どんよりとしたくらい空気」、陰鬱な空模様

snapped out of that daze 「やっと気をとりなおして」（snap out of... ：～を吹っ切る、daze：ぼーっとした状態）

"Hello!" shouted Budory.

No one came out.

"Hello!!" he yelled again at the very top of his lungs.

At that, a man stuck his big gray face out of the second-floor window directly above Budory. The lenses of his glasses glittered like stars.

"Quiet, will ya? There's a class going on up here! If you've come for something, get on in here," hollered the man before pulling his head into the window, after which there was raucous laughter in the room and the man started going on about something again in the same loud voice.

Budory plucked up his nerve, entered the building and climbed the stairs to the second floor, trying to make as little noise as possible as he walked. The door at the top of the stairs was open and an enormous room appeared right before him. The room was crammed with pupils wearing all types of clothes. There was a black wall on the opposite side of the room with lots of white lines scrawled over it, and the tall man in glasses from before was pointing to various parts of a large model of a tower and explaining something loudly to the pupils.

It only took one look at the tower for Budory to realize that this was the model of what had been called in the professor's book "The History of History." The professor laughed, took hold of a knob and turned it. The tower model made a clicking sound and turned into a bizarrely-shaped ship. When he clicked the knob around again, the model was now transformed into the shape of a huge centipede.

All the pupils cocked their head one way then the next, utterly puzzled by what they were seeing, but to Budory it all just looked incredibly intriguing.

「今日は。」ブドリは高く叫びました。誰も出てきませんでした。「今日はあ。」ブドリはあらん限り高く叫びました。するとすぐ頭の上の二階の窓から、大きな灰いろの頭が出て、めがねが二つぎらりと光りました。それから、

「今授業中だよ。やかましいやつだ。用があるならはいって来い。」とどなりつけて、すぐ顔を引っ込めますと、中では大勢でどっと笑い、その人は構わずまた何か大声でしゃべっています。ブドリはそこで思い切って、なるべく足音をたてないように二階にあがって行きますと、階段のつき当りの扉があいていて、じつに大きな教室が、ブドリのまっ正面にあらわれました。中にはさまざまの服装をした学生がぎっしりです。向うは大きな黒い壁になっていて、そこにたくさんの白い線が引いてあり、さっきのせいの高い眼がねをかけた人が、大きな櫓の形の模型を、あちこち指しながら、さっきのままの高い声で、みんなに説明して居りました。

ブドリはそれを一目見ると、ああこれは先生の本に書いてあった歴史の歴史ということの模型だなと思いました。先生は笑いながら、一つのとってを廻しました。模型はがちっと鳴って奇体な船のような形になりました。またがちっととってを廻すと、模型はこんどは大きなむかでのような形に変りました。

みんなはしきりに首をかたむけて、どうもわからんという風にしていましたが、ブドリにはただ面白かったのです。

at the very top of his lungs 「あらん限り高く」、声を限りに

hollered 「どなりつけて」、大声で叫んだ

raucous laughter 「大勢でどっと笑い」、けたたましい笑い声

plucked up his nerve 「思い切って」、勇気をふるい起こして（pluck up：奮い起こす）

centipede 「むかで」

intriguing 「面白かった」

"This diagram will make it clear," said the professor, nimbly drawing an elaborate diagram on the black wall.

He had chalk in his left hand too, and he also drew with that. The pupils copied everything diligently. As for Budory, he took the mud-stained little diary from his inside coat pocket that he had kept with him from the time he worked in the marsh paddies and copied down the diagram in it. The professor had finished his drawing and was now standing straight as a pin on the rostrum, glaring around the room at his pupils. Budory, too, had finished his drawing and was examining it when the pupil next to him yawned a big yawn.

"Um, what's the name of this professor?" asked Budory quietly.

The pupil chortled through his nose, as if making fun of Budory.

"He's the great Prof. Koobow," he said. "You really didn't know?"

The pupil looked Budory up and down, then added ...

"You really think you can draw this diagram the first time around? I've been taking this same course for six years now."

The pupil stuffed his notebook into the inside pocket of his jacket. At that moment the lights in the room flashed on. It was already evening. The great professor spoke ...

「そこでこういう図ができる。」先生は黒い壁へ別の込み入った図をどんどん書きました。左手にもチョークをもって、さっさっと書きました。学生たちもみんな一生けん命そのまねをしました。ブドリもふところから、いままで沼ばたけで持っていた汚ない手帳を出して図を書きとりました。先生はもう書いてしまって、壇の上にまっすぐに立って、じろじろ学生たちの席を見まわしています。ブドリも書いてしまって、その図を縦横から見ていますと、ブドリのとなりで一人の学生が、

「あああ。」とあくびをしました。ブドリはそっとききました。

「ね、この先生はなんて言うんですか。」

すると学生はばかにしたように鼻でわらいながら答えました。

「クーボー大博士さお前知らなかったのかい。」それからじろじろブドリのようすを見ながら、

「はじめから、この図なんか書けるもんか。ぼくでさえ同じ講義をもう六年もきいているんだ。」と言って、じぶんのノートをふところへしまってしまいました。その時教室に、ぱっと電燈がつきました。もう夕方だったのです。大博士が向こうで言いました。

diagram 「図」、図形
rostrum 「壇」、演壇
chortled through his nose 「鼻でわらいながら」

"The evening is upon us, and lectures are concluded. Those amongst you who aspire to something further, you may, as is our custom, submit your notebooks for perusal, and, you will be assigned accordingly on the basis of your answers to questions put individually to you."

The pupils gave out a yell, flapping their notebooks closed. The majority of them left just like that, but about fifty or sixty of them formed a single line in front of the professor with their notebooks open for him to examine. The professor glanced over each one, asked a question or two and wrote in chalk on their lapel, "Pass" or "Re-examine" or "E for Effort." The pupils were cringing in trepidation all the while before slipping into the corridor and shrugging their shoulders; and when they got their friends to read what the professor had written on their lapel, they either found themselves smiling in glee or frowning in misery.

The examination was soon finished, and, at last, only Budory was left. When Budory took out his little muddy diary, Prof. Koobow yawned a cavernous yawn, and, stooping down, ran an eye carefully over it. He got so close to it that it looked like he was going to swallow it up.

"Fine. This diagram is exceedingly correct," he said, taking a deep and satisfying breath. "But what's the meaning of all this other stuff? Ah, manure for the marsh paddies and horse feed, I see. Well, now answer me this. What are the various colors of smoke that emanate from the chimney of a factory?"

"Black, dark brown, yellow, gray, white, colorless," burst out Budory in a clear voice. "As well as a mixture of those."

The great professor smiled.

"Excellent that you included 'colorless.' Now, tell me about the shapes."

「いまや夕ははるかに来り、拙講もまた全課を了えた。諸君のうちの希望者は、けだしいつもの例により、そのノートをば拙者に示し、更に数箇の試問を受けて、所属を決すべきである。」学生たちはわあと叫んで、みんなばたばたノートをとじました。それからそのまま帰ってしまうものが大部分でしたが、五六十人は一列になって大博士の前をとおりながらノートを開いて見せるのでした。すると大博士はそれをちょっと見て、一言か二言質問をして、それから白墨でえりへ、「合」とか、「再来」とか「奮励」とか書くのでした。学生はその間、いかにも心配そうに首をちぢめているのでしたが、それからそっと肩をすぼめて廊下まで出て、友だちにそのしるしを読んで貰って、よろこんだりしょげたりするのでした。

　ぐんぐん試験が済んで、いよいよブドリ一人になりました。ブドリがその小さな汚ない手帳を出したとき、クーボー大博士は大きなあくびをやりながら、屈んで眼をぐっと手帳につけるようにしましたので、手帳はあぶなく大博士に吸い込まれそうになりました。

　ところが大博士は、うまそうにこくっと一つ息をして、

「よろしい。この図は非常に正しくできている。そのほかのところは、何だ、ははあ、沼ばたけのこやしのことに、馬のたべ物のことかね。では問題を答えなさい。工場の煙突から出るけむりには、どういう色の種類があるか。」

　ブドリは思わず大声に答えました。

「黒、褐、黄、灰、白、無色。それからこれらの混合です。」

　大博士はわらいました。

「無色のけむりはたいへんいい。形について言いたまえ。」

perusal 「試問」、精査

cringing in
trepidation 「心配そうに首をちぢめて」、不安に身をすくめて

yawned a cavernous
yawn 「大きなくびをやりながら」（cavernous：大洞窟のような、だだっ広い）

emanate 　（けむりが）「出る」

"If there is a large amount of smoke on a windless day, it will rise straight up, with the top end gradually spreading out. If the clouds are extremely low, the pole of smoke will rise up to the clouds, then spread to the sides. On days when the wind is blowing, the pole of smoke will rise on an angle, with its inclination determined by the extent of the wind's force. Waves or cleavages in the smoke will depend upon the wind, as well as upon the peculiarities of the smoke and the chimney themselves. If there is only very little smoke, it may take on the shape of a corkscrew; and if there is a heavy gas mixed into the smoke, it may come out of the chimney in the form of a tassel, then fall to the ground in one or any number of places."

The great professor once again smiled.

"Fine. What kind of work do you do, son?"

"I've come in search of work."

"There's a very interesting job that needs to be done here. Here's my name card. Go right away to the place I write on it."

The professor produced a name card, jotted something down on it and handed it to Budory. Budory bowed and was about to go out the door when the great professor softly whispered, "What's this? Are they burning rubbish or something?" He then gathered up his pieces of chalk, his handkerchief and books, all of which were on the table, and threw them together into his briefcase, which he slipped under his arm, before flitting right out the very same window that he had stuck his head out before. Budory, shocked, ran to the window. The great professor was already riding in a little airship that looked like a big toy, steering it over the pale-blue mist that had enveloped the town and straight into the distance. Budory stared in amazement as the great professor landed on the flat roof of a huge gray building and connected his airship onto what looked like a hook before slipping into the building and vanishing from sight.

「無風で煙が相当あれば、たての棒にもなりますが、さきはだんだんひろがります。雲の非常に低い日は、棒は雲まで昇って行って、そこから横にひろがります。風のある日は、棒は斜めになりますが、その傾きは風の程度に従います。波や幾つもきれになるのは、風のためにもよりますが、一つはけむりや煙突のもつ癖のためです。あまり煙の少ないときは、コルク抜きの形にもなり、煙も重い瓦斯がまじれば、煙突の口から房になって、一方乃至四方に落ちることもあります。」大博士はまたわらいました。

「よろしい。きみはどういう仕事をしているのか。」

「仕事をみつけに来たんです。」

「面白い仕事がある。名刺をあげるから、そこへすぐ行きなさい。」博士は名刺をとり出して、何かするする書き込んでブドリに呉れました。ブドリはおじぎをして、戸口を出て行こうとしますと、大博士はちょっと眼で答えて、

「何だ。ごみを焼いてるのかな。」と低くつぶやきながら、テーブルの上にあった鞄に、白墨のかけらや、はんけちや本や、みんな一緒に投げ込んで小脇にかかえ、さっき顔を出した窓から、プイッと外へ飛び出しました。びっくりしてブドリが窓へかけよって見ますといつか大博士は玩具のような小さな飛行船に乗って、じぶんでハンドルをとりながら、もううす青いもやのこめた町の上を、まっすぐに向うへ飛んでいるのでした。ブドリがいよいよ呆れて見ていますと、間もなく大博士は、向うの大きな灰いろの建物の平屋根に着いて船を何かかぎのようなものにつなぐと、そのままぽろっと建物の中へ入って見えなくなってしまいました。

inclination 「傾き」

cleavages 「きれ」、切れ目、裂け目

corkscrew 「コルク抜き」

tassel 「房」

flitting out 「プイッと外へ飛び出しました」、素早く外に出る

little airship 「小さな飛行船」

enveloped （もやの）「こめた」、包まれた

hook 「かぎ」

THE IHATOV BUREAU OF VOLCANOS

Budory went to the address that Prof. Koobow had written on his name card, and there he found an imposing brown building with a tall tassel-shaped pillar in the back that loomed distinctly white against the night sky. He stood in the entry hall and pushed a button that rang a bell. A man came out immediately, took the name card, glanced over it and, on the spot, led Budory to a large room straight down the corridor.

The room had the biggest table that Budory had ever seen; and sitting up right at the middle of the table was a distinguished-looking man with a clump of white hair on his head and a telephone receiver to his ear, writing something down. The moment he caught sight of Budory, he indicated that he should sit in the chair right beside him, then turned back to his writing.

A huge model map of all Ihatov, colored in beautiful colors, covered the entire right-hand side wall of the room, and all of the railroad tracks and towns and rivers and fields could be made out on it at a glance. A mountain range ran like a backbone straight down the middle of the map, and there was also a string of green mountains skirting the coast, with red and bitter-orange and yellow lights attached to the row of mountains that formed a scattering of islands branching out from it into the sea; and those lights changed colors, whirring like cicadas, and displayed numbers that appeared and disappeared in a flash. Well over a hundred black typewriter-like machines sat in three rows on shelves affixed to the wall below, all quietly humming away. Budory, forgetting himself, watched as the man laid down the receiver, and, reaching into his inside pocket, pulled out a name card holder.

五、　イーハトーブ火山局

　ブドリが、クーボー大博士から貰った名刺の宛名をたずねて、やっと着いたところは大きな茶いろの建物で、うしろには房のような形をした高い柱が夜のそらにくっきり白く立って居りました。ブドリは玄関に上って呼鈴を押しますと、すぐ人が出て来て、ブドリの出した名刺を受け取り、一目見ると、すぐブドリを突き当りの大きな室へ案内しました。そこにはいままでに見たこともないような大きなテーブルがあって、そのまん中に一人の少し髪の白くなった人のよさそうな立派な人が、きちんと座って耳に受話器をあてながら何か書いていました。そしてブドリのはいって来たのを見ると、すぐ横の椅子を指しながらまた続けて何か書きつけています。

　その室の右手の壁いっぱいに、イーハトーブ全体の地図が、美しく色どった巨きな模型に作ってあって、鉄道も町も川も野原もみんな一目でわかるようになって居り、そのまん中を走るせぼねのような山脈と、海岸に沿って縁をとったようになっている山脈、またそれから枝を出して海の中に点々の島をつくっている一列の山々には、みんな赤や橙や黄のあかりがついていて、それが代る代る色が変ったりジーと蝉のように鳴ったり、数字が現われたり消えたりしているのです。下の壁に添った棚には、黒いタイプライターのようなものが三列に百でもきかないくらい並んで、みんなしずかに動いたり鳴ったりしているのでした。ブドリがわれを忘れて見とれて居りますと、その人が受話器をことっと置いてふところから名刺入れを出して、一枚の名刺をブドリに出しながら、

"Are you Budory Goosko?" he asked, handing Budory his name card. "Here's my card."

The card read ...

NOM PENPEN
Chief Engineer
Ihatov Bureau of Volcanos

When he saw that Budory, unused to the formalities of greeting, was fidgeting about, he added politely ...

"Prof. Koobow phoned, so I have been expecting you. So, from now on I want you to work here and learn whatever you can. We just started up last year, but the work here carries a good deal of responsibility, and half of that comes from the fact that we're working atop a volcano and no one knows when it will erupt. Besides, it's the very peculiar nature of volcanic eruptions that they are not really amenable to prediction. We've got to keep our wits about us. Now, you'll be staying over there tonight, so relax and have a good rest. I'll take you around this building tomorrow."

The next morning, Budory was given a tour of every corner of the building by Chief Engineer Penpen and shown the workings of the various machines and monitoring instruments. All of them recorded and displayed graphs and figures of the state of the three-hundred-odd active and dormant volcanos of Ihatov, those that spewed out smoke and ash and sent lava flowing down their slopes, as well as those ancient ones that looked totally inactive, indicating everything from the amount of magma and gas in them to the alterations in the shape of their mountains. The models rang out with different sounds whenever there was an abrupt change in a situation.

「あなたが、グスコーブドリ君ですか。私はこう言うものです。」と言いました。見ると、イーハトーブ火山局技師ペンネンナームと書いてありました。その人はブドリの挨拶になれないでもじもじしているのを見ると、重ねて親切に言いました。

「さっきクーボー博士から電話があったのでお待ちしていました。まあこれから、ここで仕事しながらしっかり勉強してごらんなさい。ここの仕事は、去年はじまったばかりですが、じつに責任のあるもので、それに半分はいつ噴火するかわからない火山の上で仕事するものなのです。それに火山の癖というものは、なかなか学問でわかることではないのです。われわれはこれからよほどしっかりやらなければならんのです。では今晩はあっちにあなたの泊るところがありますから、そこでゆっくりお休みなさい。あしたこの建物中をすっかり案内しますから。」

次の朝、ブドリはペンネン老技師に連れられて、建物のなかを――つれて歩いて貰いさまざまの器械やしかけを詳しく教わりました。その建物のなかのすべての器械はみんなイーハトーブ中の三百幾つかの活火山や休火山に続いていて、それらの火山の煙や灰を噴いたり、熔岩を流したりしているようすは勿論、みかけはじっとしている古い火山でも、その中の熔岩や瓦斯のもようから、山の形の変りようまで、みんな数字になったり図になったりして、あらわれて来るのでした。そして烈しい変化のある度に、模型はみんな別々の音で鳴るのでした。

fidgeting about 「もじもじしている」

keep our wits about us 「よほどしっかりやらなければ」、気を引き締める

spewed out smoke and ash 「煙や灰を噴いたり」

magma 「熔岩」

to the alterations 「変りようまで」

From that day on Budory learned how to handle all of the instruments and mechanisms and how to observe the findings, working and studying night and day, throwing himself into his work heart and soul. After two years, Budory went out with his co-workers, installing monitoring instruments in any number of volcanos and repairing those instruments that were not working properly, until he knew the three-hundred-odd volcanos of Ihatov and the ins and outs of their activity as if acquiring such knowledge was his second nature.

There were, in reality, some seventy volcanos in Ihatov that spewed out smoke and lava every day, and another fifty-odd dormant ones that expelled gas and boiling water. Among the remaining one hundred sixty or seventy extinct volcanos were those that couldn't be counted on to remain that way forever.

When Budory was working alongside Chief Engineer Penpen one day, the instrument monitoring the Sanmorini Volcano on the south coast began, without warning, to stir.

"Budory," cried out Chief Engineer Penpen, "Sanmorini's been pretty quiet till today, hasn't it?"

"Yes, I've not seen Sanmorini stir until now."

"Ah, there's an eruption looming. This morning's earthquake has stirred it up. Sanmorini Township lies ten kilometers north of the mountain. An explosion now would probably knock off one-third of the mountain's northern face, sending boulders the size of cows or tables, together with fiery ash and gas, all over Sanmorini Township. We've got to drill a borehole into the side of the mountain that faces the sea to let the gas and lava out before it's too late. Let's go right now to have a look."

The two of them got ready immediately and boarded the train bound for Sanmorini.

ブドリはその日からペンネン老技師について、すべての器械の扱い方や観測のしかたを習い、夜も昼も一心に働いたり勉強したりしました。そして二年ばかりたちますとブドリはほかの人たちと一緒に、あちこちの火山へ器械を据え付けに出されたり、据え付けてある器械の悪くなったのを修繕にやられたりもするようになりましたので、もうブドリにはイーハトーブの三百幾つの火山と、その働き工合は掌の中にあるようにわかって来ました。じつにイーハトーブには七十幾つの火山が毎日煙をあげたり、熔岩を流したりしているのでしたし、五十幾つかの休火山は、いろいろな瓦斯を噴いたり、熱い湯を出したりしていました。そして残りの百六七十の死火山のうちにもいつまた何をはじめるかわからないものもあるのでした。

　ある日ブドリが老技師とならんで仕事をして居りますと、俄かにサンムトリという南の方の海岸にある火山が、むくむく器械に感じ出して来ました。老技師が叫びました。

　「ブドリ君。サンムトリは、今朝まで何もなかったね。」

　「はい、いままでサンムトリのはたらいたのを見たことがありません。」

　「ああ、これはもう噴火が近い。今朝の地震が刺戟したのだ。この山の北十キロのところにはサンムトリの市がある。今度爆発すれば、多分山は三分の一、北側をはねとばして、牛や卓子ぐらいの岩は熱い灰や瓦斯といっしょに、どしどしサンムトリ市に落ちてくる。どうでも今のうちにこの海に向いた方へボーリングを入れて傷口をこさえて、瓦斯を抜くか熔岩を出させるかしなければならない。今すぐ二人で見に行こう。」二人はすぐに支度して、サンムトリ行きの汽車に乗りました。

knew... the ins and outs of 「掌の中にあるようにわかって来ました」、一部始終を理解した

Sanmorini Volcano 「サンムトリという火山」

There's an eruption looming 「噴火が近い」

boulders 「岩」

THE SANMORINI VOLCANO

The two of them arrived in Sanmorini Township on the morning of the next day and, around noon, climbed up to the hut that housed the observation instruments near the summit of Mt. Sanmorini. The old outer rim of the crater faced the sea; and when they looked out of the window of the hut, the sea appeared like so many stripes of blue and gray, and the steamer gliding over those wavy stripes sent up plumes of black smoke as it left a silver channel in its wake.

The chief engineer calmly examined all of the monitoring instruments.

"How many days do you think it will take this mountain to erupt?" he asked Budory.

"Less than a month, I'd say, sir."

"Less than a month? Less than ten days, I'd say. If we don't engineer this right away, there'll be no going back. It seems to me that the weakest spot on this mountain where it faces the sea is over there."

The chief engineer pointed to a light-green patch of grassland above a ravine on the slope of the mountain. The shadow of a cloud was skating easily over it, turning it from green to blue.

"There are only two layers of lava there. In addition, there's a layer of soft volcanic ash and lapilli. Besides, a great road from the stock farm leading up there means that we can transport our materials without difficulty. I'll radio the engineering brigade and call them in."

The chief engineer began to busy himself with a call to headquarters, when there was a faint grumbling sound under their feet and the observation hut momentarily creaked and squeaked. The chief engineer moved away from the monitoring instruments.

六、 サンムトリ火山

　二人は次の朝、サンムトリの市に着き、ひるごろサンムトリ火山の頂近く、観測器械を置いてある小屋に登りました。そこは、サンムトリ山の古い噴火口の外輪山が、海の方へ向いて欠けた所で、その小屋の窓からながめますと、海は青や灰いろの幾つもの縞になって見え、その中を汽船は黒いけむりを吐き、銀いろの水脈を引いていくつも滑って居るのでした。

　老技師はしずかにすべての観測機を調べ、それからブドリに言いました。

　「きみはこの山はあと何日ぐらいで噴火すると思うか。」

　「一月はもたないと思います。」

　「一月はもたない。もう十日ももたない。早く工作をしてしまわないと、取り返しのつかないことになる。私はこの山の海に向いた方では、あすこがいちばん弱いと思う。」老技師は山腹の谷の上のうす緑の草地を指さしました。そこを雲の影がしずかに青く滑っているのでした。

　「あすこには熔岩の層が二つしかない。あとは柔らかな火山灰と火山礫の層だ。それにあすこまでは牧場の道も立派にあるから、材料を運ぶことも造作ない。ぼくは工作隊を申請しよう。」老技師は忙しく局へ発信をはじめました。その時脚の下では、つぶやくような微かな音がして、観測小屋はしばらくぎしぎし軋みました。老技師は機械をはなれました。

ravine on the slope of the mountain 「山腹の谷」、峡谷、渓谷

lapilli 「火山礫」。火山噴火により生じた火山岩片

engineering brigade 「工作隊」（brigade：隊）

"Headquarters are sending out the engineering brigade right away. Might be more appropriate to call them the suicide brigade. I've never been involved in any job more dangerous than this."

"Do you think we can manage it in ten days?"

"I do. The equipment will be up here from the Sanmorini Power Plant in three days, and it'll take, I'd say, another five to string the wiring."

He counted with his fingers while pondering something, then, appearing relieved, spoke calmly again.

"Anyway, Budory, how about brewing up some tea. The view's just so magnificent from here."

Budory lit the alcohol lamp that they had brought with them and began to boil up some water. Clouds began to appear in the sky, and the sea had become a cheerless gray as the sun seemed to fall away and white crests rolled, one after the other, against the foot of the mountain.

All of a sudden, a weirdly shaped little airship that Budory had seen before appeared before his eyes. The chief engineer bolted up.

"Ah, Prof. Koobow's here," he said.

Budory followed him out of the hut. The airship had already landed on top of a massive rock wall to the left of the hut, and the tall Prof. Koobow was nimbly hopping out of it. For a while he searched the area on top of the rock for a big fissure, then, finding it, promptly anchored down the airship by driving a screw into it.

"I've come for a cup of tea," said the great professor, grinning. "Is there a lot of trembling and shaking going on?"

"Not much yet," answered the chief engineer. "However, rocks are crumbling off the cliff face above here."

「局からすぐ工作隊を出すそうだ。工作隊といっても半分決死隊だ。私はいままでに、こんな危険に迫った仕事をしたことがない。」

「十日のうちにできるでしょうか。」

「きっとできる。装置には三日、サンムトリ市の発電所から、電線を引いてくるには五日かかるな。」

技師はしばらく指を折って考えていましたが、やがて安心したようにまたしずかに言いました。

「とにかくブドリ君。一つ茶をわかして呑もうではないか。あんまりいい景色だから。」

ブドリは持って来たアルコールランプに火を入れて茶をわかしはじめました。空にはだんだん雲が出て、それに日ももう落ちたのか、海はさびしい灰いろに変り、たくさんの白い波がしらは、一せいに火山の裾に寄せて来ました。

ふとブドリはすぐ眼の前にいつか見たことのあるおかしな形の小さな飛行船が飛んでいるのを見つけました。老技師もはねあがりました。

「あ、クーボー君がやって来た。」

ブドリも続いて小屋をとび出しました。飛行船はもう小屋の左側の大きな岩の壁の上にとまって中からせいの高いクーボー大博士がひらりと飛び下りていました。博士はしばらくその辺の岩の大きなさけ目をさがしていましたが、やっとそれを見つけたと見えて、手早くねじをしめて飛行船をつなぎました。

「お茶をよばれに来たよ。ゆれるかい。」大博士はにやにやわらって言いました。老技師が答えました。

「まだそんなでない。けれどもどうも岩がぼろぼろ上から落ちているらしいんだ。」

suicide brigade 「決死隊」

brewing up some tea 「茶をわかして」

nimbly 「ひらりと」、すばやく

fissure 「さけ目」

driving a screw into it 「ねじをしめて」

It was precisely then … the mountain groaned, as if in fury, and everything seemed to turn blue in front of Budory's eyes. The mountain was now ferociously shaking and trembling. When he looked down, he saw both Prof. Koobow and the chief engineer crouched down, clinging to the ground. The airship was pitching and rolling like a ship on waves.

When the earthquake finally ceased, Prof. Koobow stood up and dashed into the hut. The kettle had been knocked over, and the alcohol in the lamp was glowing blue. Prof. Koobow examined the monitoring instruments thoroughly, after which he entered into a long discussion with the chief engineer.

"Whatever the case may be," he said, "we've got to build our tidal power stations and get them working by next year. If we do that, come what may, we'll be able to take on any challenge and Budory here will have all the manure he needs to rain over his marsh paddies."

"And he won't have to worry ever again about droughts," said Chief Engineer Penpen.

Budory's heart leapt for joy. In fact, he thought it was dancing right up the side of the mountain! But the mountain at that moment again shook and quaked violently, and Budory was thrown to the floor.

"We can do it. We can do it!" said the great professor, adding, "They no doubt felt that in Sanmorini Township as well."

"What just happened now," said the chief engineer, "is that below our feet, about one kilometer to the north of here, seven hundred meters below the surface of the Earth, a lump of rock about sixty or seventy times the size of this hut fell into a pool of magma. But before the crust lets gas fly out of it, one or two hundred rocks like that will be holding it all inside first."

ちょうどその時、山は俄かに怒ったように鳴り出し、ブドリは眼の前が青くなったように思いました。山はぐらぐら続けてゆれました。見るとクーボー大博士も老技師もしゃがんで岩へしがみついていましたし、飛行船も大きな波に乗った船のようにゆっくりゆれて居りました。地震はやっとやみクーボー大博士は、起きあがってすたすたと小屋へ入って行きました。中ではお茶がひっくり返って、アルコールが青くぽかぽか燃えていました。クーボー大博士は機械をすっかり調べて、それから老技師といろいろ談しました。そしてしまいに言いました。

　「もうどうしても来年は潮汐発電所を全部作ってしまわなければならない。それができれば今度のような場合にもその日のうちに仕事ができるし、ブドリ君が言っている沼ばたけの肥料も降らせられるんだ。」

　「早魃だってちっともこわくなくなるからな。」ペンネン技師も言いました。ブドリは胸がわくわくしました。山まで踊りあがっているように思いました。じっさい山は、その時烈しくゆれ出して、ブドリは床へ投げ出されていたのです。大博士が言いました。

　「やるぞ、やるぞ。いまのはサンムトリの市へもかなり感じたにちがいない。」

　老技師が言いました。

　「今のはぼくらの足もとから、北へ一キロばかり地表下七百米ぐらいの所で、この小屋の六七十倍ぐらいの岩の塊が熔岩の中へ落ち込んだらしいのだ。ところが瓦斯がいよいよ最後の岩の皮をはね飛ばすまでにはそんな塊を百も二百も、じぶんのからだの中にとらなければならない。」

groaned, as if in fury
「怒ったように鳴り出し」

pitching and rolling
「ゆっくりゆれて」、前後左右にゆれて。pitching は「縦揺れ」、rolling は「横揺れ」

tidal power stations
「潮汐発電所」

The great professor was plunged into thought.

"Very well," he finally said. "I will take my leave now."

Having said that, he left the hut and, in a flash, nimbly leapt into his airship. The chief engineer and Budory watched as the great professor waved a light two or three times in parting, circled the mountain and flew away.

Chief Engineer Penpen and Budory returned to the hut, taking turns sleeping and observing.

When, at dawn, the engineering brigade arrived at the foot of the mountain, the chief engineer left Budory alone in the hut and climbed down to the grassland that he had pointed to the day before. The voices of all the men and the clanking of the iron and steel of the materials they had brought sailed up the slopes on the wind, making it sound like they were already on the mountain.

Chief Engineer Penpen made sure that everyone was constantly informed about the progress of the work, keeping an eye all the while on the pressure of the gas and any changes in the shape of the mountain. For three days the earth there quaked and rumbled, and neither Budory up above nor those down below could get more than a wink of sleep. The chief engineer radioed up to Budory on the morning of the fourth day.

"That Budory? We're all ready. Get yourself down here right away. Check the monitors and leave them on, and bring all your graphs with you. That hut's going to disappear from the face of the Earth this afternoon."

大博士はしばらく考えていましたが、「そうだ、僕はこれで失敬しよう。」と言って小屋を出て、いつかひらりと船に乗ってしまいました。老技師とブドリは、大博士があかりを二三度振って挨拶しながら山をまわって向うへ行くのを見送ってまた小屋に入り、かわるがわる眠ったり観測したりしました。そして暁方 麓へ工作隊がつきますと、老技師はブドリを一人小屋に残して、昨日指さしたあの草地まで降りて行きました。みんなの声や、鉄の材料の触れ合う音は、下から風が吹き上げるときは、手にとるように聴えました。ペンネン技師からはひっきりなしに、向うの仕事の進み工合も知らせてよこし、瓦斯の圧力や山の形の変りようも尋ねて来ました。それから三日の間は、はげしい地震や地鳴りのなかでブドリの方も、麓の方もほとんど眠るひまさえありませんでした。その四日目の午后、老技師からの発信が言ってきました。

　「ブドリ君だな。すっかり支度ができた。急いで降りてきたまえ。観測の器械は一ぺん調べてそのままにして、表は全部持ってくるのだ。もうその小屋は今日の午后にはなくなるんだから。」

was plunged into thought 「しばらく考えていました」、物思いに沈んでいた

take my leave 「失敬しよう」、いとまを告げる

Budory did exactly as he was told and descended the mountain. Huge pieces of iron and steel that had been kept in storage at headquarters had gone into making a tower, and machines were there just waiting to be wired up. Chief Engineer Penpen's cheeks were sunken in, and the faces of the engineers of the engineering brigade had turned pale. But their eyes lit up when they saw Budory, and they greeted him with big smiles.

"Well, let's pull out. Everybody get ready and hop into the cars," said the chief engineer.

All of the engineers hurried into twenty cars that raced along the foot of the mountain in a single line toward Sanmorini Township. Just as they were about halfway between the mountain and the township, the chief engineer stopped the cars.

"Pitch your tents here, men!" he said. "We all need some sleep."

All of them collapsed into a deep sleep without a word of objection. The next afternoon, the chief engineer put down his radio earphones and cried out ...

"The wires are in place! Budory, this is it!"

He flicked the switch. Budory and the others left their tents and gazed at a point halfway up the mountain. The meadow leading up to the mountain was blanketed in white lilies, and the peak rose above it, a majestic blue tower.

All of a sudden, the left base of the mountain swayed and quaked, and a black column of smoke emerged and rose straight up to the sky, taking on a strange mushroom-like form and giving off golden lava at its base, gleaming the moment it appeared. The lava took on a fan shape before their eyes as it flowed into the sea. Now the earth shook violently, the blanket of lilies pitched and rolled, and a thundering boom, strong enough to knock them all off their feet, hit them, with a monstrous gust of wind following in its wake.

ブドリはすっかり言われた通りにして山を下りて行きました。そこにはいままで局の倉庫にあった大きな鉄材が、すっかり櫓に組み立っていて、いろいろな機械はもう電流さえ来ればすぐに働き出すばかりになっていました。ペンネン技師の頬はげっそり落ち、工作隊の人たちも青ざめて眼ばかり光らせながら、それでもみんな笑ってブドリに挨拶しました。老技師が言いました。

「では引き上げよう。みんな支度して車に乗り給え。」みんなは大急ぎで二十台の自動車に乗りました。車は列になって山の裾を一散にサンムトリの市に走りました。丁度山と市とのまん中ごろで技師は自動車をとめさせました。

「ここへ天幕を張り給え。そしてみんなで眠るんだ。」

みんなは、物を一言も言えずにその通りにして倒れるように睡ってしまいました。

その午后、老技師は受話器を置いて叫びました。

「さあ電線は届いたぞ。ブドリ君、始めるよ。」老技師はスイッチを入れました。ブドリたちは、天幕の外に出て、サンムトリの中腹を見つめました。野原には、白百合がいちめん咲き、その向うにサンムトリが青くひっそり立っていました。

俄かにサンムトリの左の裾がぐらぐらっとゆれまっ黒なけむりがぱっと立ったと思うとまっすぐに天にのぼって行って、おかしなきのこの形になり、その足もとから黄金色の熔岩がきらきら流れ出して、見るまにずうっと扇形にひろがりながら海へ入りました。と思うと地面は烈しくぐらぐらゆれ、百合の花もいちめんゆれ、それからごうっというような大きな音が、みんなを倒すくらい強くやってきました。それから風がどうっと吹いて行きました。

"Hell yes! We've done it!" cried everyone, pointing to the mountain.

Smoke from Mt. Sanmorini spread out, breaking apart throughout the sky, the sky was soon pitch black, and hot little stones and pebbles rained down on them. They all went anxiously into the tents.

"Budory," said Chief Engineer Penpen, "it's gone well. The danger has completely passed. The only thing the township has to worry about now is a bit of ash falling on it."

The little stones and pebbles soon turned into ash, then that too thinned out, and everyone rushed out of the tents. The entire meadow was now dark gray, covered by ash about three centimeters deep, all of the lilies were crushed and buried in ash, and the sky had taken on a strange green tint. A little bulge had appeared at the foot of Mt. Sanmorini, and from that a column of gray smoke was rising rapidly upwards.

That evening, all of the people climbed back up the mountain, stepping on ash, little rocks and pebbles, and, after installing new monitoring instruments, made their way back on home.

A SEA OF CLOUDS

As many as two hundred tidal power stations were built along the seacoast of Ihatov during the following four years, just as Prof. Koobow had planned. Observation huts and towers painted white were erected, one after the other, on the volcanos encircling Ihatov.

Budory, who now had a good grounding in engineering, spent most of his year making the rounds from volcano to volcano, fixing up equipment on those that were in danger of erupting.

「やったやった。」とみんなはそっちに手を延して高く叫びました。この時サンムトリの煙は、崩れるようにそらいっぱいひろがって来ましたが、忽ちそらはまっ暗になって、熱いこいしがぱらぱらぱらぱら降ってきました。みんなは天幕の中にはいって心配そうにしていましたが、ペンネン技師は、時計を見ながら、

　「ブドリ君、うまく行った。危険はもう全くない。市の方へは灰をすこし降らせるだけだろう。」と言いました。こいしはだんだん灰にかわりました。それもまもなく薄くなってみんなはまた天幕の外へ飛び出しました。野原はまるで一めん鼠いろになって、灰はちょっとばかり積り、百合の花はみんな折れて灰に埋まり、空は変に緑いろでした。そしてサンムトリの裾には小さな瘤ができて、そこから灰いろの煙が、まだどんどん登って居りました。

　その夕方みんなは、灰やこいしを踏んで、もう一度山へのぼって、新らしい観測の機械を据え着けて帰りました。

七、　雲の海

　それから四年の間に、クーボー大博士の計画通り、潮汐発電所は、イーハトーブの海岸に沿って、二百も配置されました。イーハトーブをめぐる火山には、観測小屋といっしょに、白く塗られた鉄の櫓が順々に建ちました。

　ブドリは技師心得になって、一年の大部分は火山から火山と廻ってあるいたり、危くなった火山を工作したりしていました。

pebbles　小石

rained down　「ぱらぱらぱらぱら降ってきました」、雨のように降り注いだ

thinned out　「薄くなって」

In the spring of the following year, the Ihatov Bureau of Volcanos put up a poster in the villages and towns.

Nitrogenous fertilizer to be released from the sky.
Ammonium nitrate will be rained upon your paddies and your vegetable fields together with the summer rains. Those people using fertilizer please compensate suitably for this in your calculations. The amount is 120 kilograms within a one hundred meter radius. We shall also be providing some rain.

In case of drought, we will be able to provide at least enough rain so that your crop will not die, so even those who have not planted until now due to lack of water may plant this year without the slightest qualms!

June of the next year found Budory in the hut atop Mt. Ihatov, the volcano in the very middle of lhatov. A gray sea of clouds spread below him. The peaks of other volcanos in and around Ihatov stood out like black islands. A single airship was flying from peak to peak right above the clouds, as if forming bridges between them, with smoke white as snow puffing from its tail. With time, the smoke gradually thickened, and its outlines sharpened as it noiselessly landed on the sea of clouds below; and, before long, there was a gigantic pale-white radiant net stretching from mountain to mountain. Having cast this net of smoke, the airship described a circle in the air, as if in greeting, and finally, with its nose angled downward, sunk easily into the clouds.

The radio earphones buzzed. It was Chief Engineer Penpen speaking.

"My airship's back safely. Everything down below is in place. It's raining cats and dogs. Now's the time. Switch it on."

次の年の春、イーハトーブの火山局では、次のような
ポスターを村や町へ張りました。

「窒素肥料を降らせます。

　　今年の夏、雨といっしょに、硝酸アムモニアをみ
なさんの沼ばたけや蔬菜ばたけに降らせますから、肥
料を使う方は、その分を入れて計算してください。分
量は百メートル四方につき百二十キログラムです。
雨もすこしは降らせます。

　　旱魃の際には、とにかく作物の枯れないぐらいの
雨は降らせることができますから、いままで水が来な
くなって作付しなかった沼ばたけも、今年は心配せず
に植え付けてください。」

　その年の六月、ブドリはイーハトーブのまん中にあた
るイーハトーブ火山の頂上の小屋に居りました。下はい
ちめん灰いろをした雲の海でした。そのあちこちからイー
ハトーブ中の火山のいただきが、ちょうど島のように黒
く出て居りました。その雲のすぐ上を一隻の飛行船が、
船尾からまっ白な煙を噴いて一つの峯から一つの峯へ
ちょうど橋をかけるように飛びまわっていました。その
けむりは、時間がたつほどだんだん太くはっきりなって
しずかに下の雲の海に落ちかぶさり、まもなく、いちめ
んの雲の海にはうす白く光る大きな網が、山から山へ張
り互されました。いつか飛行船はけむりを納めて、しば
らく挨拶するように輪を描いていましたが、やがて船首
を垂れてしずかに雲の中へ沈んで行ってしまいました。
受話器がジーと鳴りました。ペンネン技師の声でした。

　「飛行船はいま帰って来た。下の方の支度はすっかりい
い。雨はざあざあ降っている。もうよかろうと思う。は
じめてくれ給え。」

Nitrogenous fertilizer
「窒素肥料」

Ammonium nitrate
「硝酸アンモニア」

*compensate suitably
for this in your
calculations* 「その分を
入れて計算して」、その分
を計算して適切に補う

qualms 「心配」

raining cats and
dogs 「雨はざあざあ
降っている」、雨が土砂降
りで

Budory pushed a button. In an instant, the net of smoke sparkled a beautiful pink and blue and purple, flickering on and off so brightly as to dazzle the eyes. Budory was spellbound by the sight. As day gave way to night and the lights in the sea of clouds went out, everything turned a shade of gray, now light, now dark.

The earphones buzzed again.

"The ammonium nitrate is all mixed in with the rain. The amount is just about right, too. The spread also seems good. Another four hours of doing this and this region will have had enough for this month. Keep doing what you're doing."

Budory was so happy he felt like jumping for joy.

The owner of the paddies with the old-time red beard and the man who wondered whether petrol would act as a fertilizer were listening with glee to the sound of the rain coming from the clouds. The next day they would no doubt not believe their eyes when they stroked their oryza stalks that had suddenly come up green. They gazed as if in a dream at the cloud cover that alternated between a blanket of total darkness and a sheet of soft radiance. But the short summer night seemed to be breaking, and the eastern edge of the sea of clouds shone dim and yellow amidst flashes of lightning.

It was the light of the moon, a huge yellow moon slowly rising … and when the clouds shone blue, the moon's face was strangely whitish, and when the clouds shone pink, it looked like it was smiling. Budory couldn't remember who he was or what he was doing there. All he could do was gaze blankly at what was unfolding before his eyes.

The earphones buzzed again.

ブドリはぼたんを押しました。見る見るさっきのけむりの網は、美しい桃いろや青や紫に、パッパッと眼もさめるようにかがやきながら、点いたり消えたりしました。ブドリはまるでうっとりとしてそれに見とれました。そのうちにだんだん日は暮れて、雲の海もあかりが消えたときは、灰いろか鼠いろかわからないようになりました。

受話器が鳴りました。

「硝酸アムモニアはもう雨の中へでてきている。量もこれぐらいならちょうどいい。移動のぐあいもいいらしい。あと四時間やれば、もうこの地方は今月中は沢山だろう。つづけてやってくれたまえ。」

ブドリはもううれしくってはね上りたいくらいでした。この雲の下で昔の赤鬚の主人もとなりの石油がこやしになるかと言った人も、みんなよろこんで雨の音を聞いている。そしてあすの朝は、見違えるように緑いろになったオリザの株を手で撫でたりするだろう、まるで夢のようだと思いながら雲のまっくらになったり、また美しく輝いたりするのを眺めて居ました。ところが短い夏の夜はもう明けるらしかったのです。電光の合間に、東の雲の海のはてがぼんやり黄ばんでいるのでした。

ところがそれは月が出るのでした。大きな黄いろな月がしずかに登るってくるのでした。そして雲が青く光るときは変に白っぽく見え、桃いろに光るときは何かわらっているように見えるのでした。ブドリは、もうじぶんが誰なのか何をしているのか忘れてしまって、ただぼんやりそれをみつめていました。受話器がジーと鳴りました。

day gave way to
night 「だんだん日は暮れて」(give way to... :
～に取って代わられる)

whitish 「白っぽく」

what was unfolding
before his eyes 目
の前で展開すること
(unfold：展開する、打ち
明ける)

"There's a lot of thunder down here. The net seems to have torn away in some places. If we keep making such a racket, tomorrow's papers are bound to give us hell, so let's call it a day for now."

Budory put down the earphones and pricked up his ears. The sea of clouds was certainly muttering and murmuring. Listening even more intently to the sound, he could tell that it was being produced by the cracks and rolls of thunderbolts.

Budory pressed the button off. The clouds were now instantly illuminated by the light of the moon alone as they continued to sail in silence toward the north. Budory wrapped himself in his blanket and was soon lost to sleep.

FALL

It may have been partially due to the weather, but the crop harvest that year was the best in ten years, and the Bureau of Volcanos was showered with letters of appreciation and support from every corner of Ihatov. For the first time in his life Budory felt that he had something to live for.

One day after harvest time, however, Budory was passing a little village set among paddies on his way back from a visit to Mt. Tacina. He stopped in a general store where they sold everything from soup to nuts. It was just about noon and he wanted to buy some vitamin tablets.

"Do you have tablets?" he asked.

Three barefoot men were in the store, their eyes bright red from drinking. One of them stood up.

「こっちでは大分雷が鳴りだして来た。網があちこちちぎれたらしい。あんまり鳴らすとあしたの新聞が悪口を言うからもう十分ばかりでやめよう。」

ブドリは受話器を置いて耳をすましました。雲の海はあっちでもこっちでもぶつぶつぶつぶつ呟いているのです。よく気をつけて聞くとやっぱりそれはきれぎれの雷の音でした。ブドリはスイッチを切りました。俄かに月のあかりだけになった雲の海は、やっぱりしずかに北へ流れています。ブドリは毛布をからだに巻いてぐっすり睡りました。

八、　秋

　その年の農作物の収穫は、気候のせいもありましたが、十年の間にもなかったほど、よく出来ましたので、火山局にはあっちからもこっちからも感謝状や激励の手紙が届きました。ブドリははじめてほんとうに生きた甲斐があるように思いました。

　ところがある日、ブドリがタチナという火山へ行った帰り、とりいれの済んでがらんとした沼ばたけの中の小さな村を通りかかりました。ちょうどひるころなので、パンを買おうと思って、一軒の雑貨や菓子を売っている店へ寄って、

　「パンはありませんか。」とききました。すると、そこには三人のはだしの人たちが、眼をまっ赤にして酒を呑んで居りましたが、一人が立ち上って、

making such a racket 「あんまり鳴らすと」。racketはここでは「騒音」の意味で、make a racket で「大騒ぎををする」

are bound to... 　〜するにちがいない

give us hell 「悪口を言う」、ひどく叱る

call it a day 「もうやめよう」、終わりにする、切りあげる

pricked up his ears 「耳をすました」

muttering and murmuring 「ぶつぶつぶつぶつ呟いている」

cracks and rolls of thunderbolts 「きれぎれの雷の音」、雷鳴と稲妻

(from) soup to nuts 「雑貨や菓子を売っている店」。「品揃えなどが何から何まで」、「初めから終わりまで」という意味がある

vitamin tablets 　原作の「パン」を vitamin tablets（ビタミン錠）と訳しているのは、「パン」と「石盤」を掛けたジョークを英語で表現することができないため。tablets you can swallow（錠剤）と tablets you write on（石盤）を掛けて日本語のジョークを英語で tablets を使って表現している

"Yeah, we got tablets," he said, "but they ain't tablets you can swallow. They're tablets you write on."

The other men ogled Budory with funny looks and burst out laughing. Budory, offended, shot outside. A tall man with a crewcut walked up to him.

"Hey, you!" he said. "You're that Budory guy who rained down all that dung stuff with that electric thing, ain't ya?"

"That's right," said Budory casually.

"Hey, Budory from the volcano bureau's here!" hollered the man. "Everybody get over here!"

That brought eighteen farmers from the store and the nearby fields, all of them guffawing and roaring with laughter.

"God damn you!" said one of them. "'Cause of your stupid damn electric thing, all of our oryza plants fell down. What the hell did you think you were doin', eh?"

"Fell down? Didn't you people see the posters we put up in the spring?"

"God damn you!" said one of the men, knocking Budory's hat off his head.

They then all closed in on Budory, beating him up and stomping on him. It wasn't long before Budory was flat on the ground, unconscious.

「パンはあるが、どうも食われないパンでな。石盤だもな。」とおかしなことを言いますと、みんなは面白そうにブドリの顔を見てどっと笑いました。ブドリはいやになって、ぷいっと表へ出ましたら、向うから髪を角刈りにしたせいの高い男が来て、いきなり、

「おい、お前、今年の夏、電気でこやし降らせたブドリだな。」と言いました。

「そうだ。」ブドリは何気なく答えました。その男は高く叫びました。

「火山局のブドリが来たぞ。みんな集れ。」

すると今の家（うち）の中やそこらの畑から、十八人の百姓たちが、げらげらわらってかけて来ました。

「この野郎、きさまの電気のお蔭で、おいらのオリザ、みんな倒れてしまったぞ。何してあんなまねしたんだ。」一人が言いました。

ブドリはしずかに言いました。

「倒れるなんて、きみらは春に出したポスターを見なかったのか。」

「何この野郎。」いきなり一人がブドリの帽子を叩（たた）き落しました。それからみんなは寄ってたかってブドリをなぐったりふんだりしました。ブドリはとうとう何が何だかわからなくなって倒れてしまいました。

ogled... with funny looks 「面白そうに〜を見て」（ogle...：〜をジロジロ見る）

guffawing and roaring with laughter 「げらげらわらって」、大声でばか笑いして

closed in on... 「寄ってたかって」、〜を包囲して

flat on the ground, unconscious 「何が何だかわからなくなって倒れてしまいました」、気を失って地面に倒れてしまった

When he came to, he was in a white bed in what looked like a hospital. There were many letters and telegrams expressing sympathy by his pillow. Budory was hurting all over, his whole body felt very hot, and he couldn't move. But a week later he was fully recovered. The paper had reported that the oryza plants had fallen down because an agricultural engineer had given the wrong instructions on how much fertilizer to use but had blamed the whole thing on the volcano bureau to cover up his blunder. When Budory read this, all he could do was laugh to himself.

The hospital caretaker visited him the next day.

"A lady by the name of Neri has come to see you," he said.

Budory couldn't believe his ears. The next thing he knew, a tan woman looking like a farmer's wife timidly entered the room. Though she looked like a different person, it was definitely his little sister Neri who had been snatched from the house in the woods by a man. They remained silent for a time, until Budory spoke up and asked her what had happened to her after that. Speaking in her rustic Ihatov accent, Neri little by little told him everything. Three days after abducting her, the man seemed to conclude that she wasn't worth the trouble, left her at a small stock farm in the district and vanished into thin air.

気がついて見るとブドリはどこかの病院らしい室の白いベッドに寝ていました。枕もとには見舞いの電報や、たくさんの手紙がありました。ブドリのからだ中は痛くて熱く、動くことができませんでした。けれどもそれから一週間ばかりたちますと、もうブドリはもとの元気になっていました。そして新聞で、あのときの出来事は、肥料の入れ様をまちがって教えた農業技師が、オリザの倒れたのをみんな火山局のせいにして、ごまかしていたためだということを読んで、大きな声で一人で笑いました。その次の日の午后、病院の小使が入って来て、

　「ネリというご婦人のお方が訪ねておいでになりました。」と言いました。ブドリは夢ではないかと思いましたら、まもなく一人の日に焼けた百姓のおかみさんのような人が、おずおずと入って来ました。それはまるで変ってはいましたが、あの森の中から誰かにつれて行かれたネリだったのです。二人はしばらく物も言えませんでしたが、やっとブドリが、その後のことをたずねますと、ネリもぼつぼつとイーハトーブの百姓のことばで、今までのことを談しました。ネリを連れて行ったあの男は、三日ばかりの後、面倒臭くなったのかある小さな牧場の近くへネリを残してどこかへ行ってしまったのでした。

cover up his blunder
「ごまかしていた」
(blunder：大しくじり、不注意な間違い)

abducting 「連れて行った」、誘拐する

stock farm 「牧場」
(stock：家畜)

vanished into thin air
「どこかへ行ってしまった」
(thin air：どこだかわからない場所)

She had wandered all around there bawling her eyes out, when the owner of the farm took pity on her and brought her home, putting her to work babysitting their newborn child. It wasn't long before Neri was doing various jobs around the farm, and, a few years ago, she married the farmer's eldest son. She explained that, thanks to the fertilizer that had rained down this year, they didn't have to carry dung to faraway fields like always, and they were able to use it on nearby turnip fields instead, and the corn crop that was cultivated in the faraway fields came good, and everyone in the house was very happy. She had gone any number of times with the farmer's son back to the old forest, but their house was in ruins and she didn't know where Budory had gone, and she always came back heartbroken, but because her husband had read in the newspaper the day before of how Budory had been hurt, she was able to visit him now.

Neri left, with Budory promising to go to her home to thank everyone.

CARBONADO ISLAND

The following five years brought only happiness to Budory. He often went back to the house of the man with the red beard to express thanks to him.

The man had put on some years but was still spry and full of vigor. He now bred longhair rabbits and had over a thousand of them, and he grew red kale in his fields. He hadn't given up his old speculating, but his life was better now than it had ever been.

ネリがそこらを泣いて歩いていますと、その牧場の主人が可哀そうに思って家へ入れて赤ん坊のお守をさせたりしていましたが、だんだんネリは何でも働けるようになったのでとうとう三四年前にその小さな牧場の一番上の息子と結婚したというのでした。そして今年は肥料も降ったので、いつもなら廐肥を遠くの畑まで運び出さなければならず、大へん難儀したのを、近くのかぶらの畑へみんな入れたし、遠くの玉蜀黍もよくできたので、家じゅうみんな悦んでいるというようなことも言いました。またあの森の中へ主人の息子といっしょに何べんも行って見たけれども、家はすっかり壊れていたし、ブドリはどこへ行ったかわからないのでいつもがっかりして帰っていたら、昨日新聞で主人がブドリのけがをしたことを読んだのでやっとこっちへ訪ねて来たということも言いました。ブドリは、直ったらきっとその家へ訪ねて行ってお礼を言う約束をしてネリを帰しました。

九、 カルボナード島

それからの五年は、ブドリにはほんとうに楽しいものでした。赤鬚の主人の家にも何べんもお礼に行きました。

もうよほど年は老っていましたが、やはり非常な元気で、こんどは毛の長い兎を千疋以上飼ったり、赤い甘藍ばかり畑に作ったり、相変らずの山師はやっていましたが、暮しはずうっといいようでした。

bawling her eyes out 「泣いて」、大声で泣いて、泣きわめいて

turnip fields 「かぶらの畑」

CARBONADO ISLAND 「カルボナード島」

spry 「元気で」

red kale 「赤い甘藍」、レッドケール

Neri gave birth to an adorable baby boy. She dressed him up to look like a little farm boy and sometimes took him, with her husband, to Budory's house to stay overnight.

One day, a man who had worked with Budory when he was raising silkworms came to visit him with the news that his parents' grave was under an immense Japanese nutmeg tree at the very edge of the forest. At the time he had found their cold bodies when walking about the forest inspecting trees and had secretly buried them without telling Budory, placing the branch of a birch tree over the grave. Budory lost no time taking Neri there, putting up a gravestone made of white limestone. He never failed to visit the gravesite whenever he was nearby.

Budory finally turned twenty-seven. It looked as if another cold winter was about to be upon them. The people at the weather station had predicted as much that February, judging by the degree of sunlight and the condition of the ice in the northern seas. Each day confirmed this. The magnolia trees did not bloom, and May saw as many as ten days of sleet. Everyone was filled with trepidation, recalling the disastrous harvests of the past. Prof. Koobow spoke often with weather experts and agricultural engineers, writing his opinions in the newspaper, but no one knew what to do, in the end, about the approaching cold summer.

ネリには、可愛らしい男の子が生れました。冬に仕事がひまになると、ネリはその子にすっかりこどもの百姓のようなかたちをさせて、主人といっしょに、ブドリの家に訪ねて来て、泊って行ったりするのでした。

ある日、ブドリのところへ、昔てぐす飼いの男にブドリといっしょに使われていた人が訪ねて来て、ブドリたちのお父さんのお墓が森のいちばんはずれの大きな榧（かや）の木の下にあるということを教えて行きました。それは、はじめ、てぐす飼いの男が森に来て、森じゅうの樹（き）を見てあるいたとき、ブドリのお父さんたちの冷くなったからだを見附けて、ブドリに知らせないように、そっと土に埋（うず）めて、上へ一本の樺（かば）の枝をたてて置いたというのでした。ブドリは、すぐネリたちをつれてそこへ行って、白い石灰岩の墓をたてて、それからもその辺を通るたびにいつも寄ってくるのでした。

そしてちょうどブドリが二十七の年でした。どうもあの恐ろしい寒い気候がまた来るような模様でした。測候所では、太陽の調子や北の方の海の氷の様子からその年の二月にみんなへそれを予報しました。それが一足ずつだんだん本当になってこぶしの花が咲かなかったり、五月に十日もみぞれが降ったりしますと、みんなはもう、この前の凶作を思い出して生きたそらもありませんでした。クーボー大博士も、たびたび気象や農業の技師たちと相談したり、意見を新聞へ出したりしましたが、やっぱりこの烈（はげ）しい寒さだけはどうともできないようすでした。

Japanese nutmeg tree 「榧（かや）の木」

their cold bodies 「冷たくなったからだ」、冷たくなった亡骸

with trepidation 「生きたそらもありません」、生きた心地もしない（trepidation：恐怖、おびえ）

The young oryza plants were still yellow and many trees had sprouted no leaves even by the beginning of June. Budory wasn't about to take the situation lying down. If things continued in this way, there would be countless people in the forests and fields suffering the same fate that his family had suffered years before. He spent night after night plunged into thought, often not even bothering to eat. One evening, he went to see Prof. Koobow at his home.

"Professor, if the amount of carbon dioxide increases in the air, it will get warmer, won't it?"

"Yes, that's what would happen. After all, it's said that the temperature since the Earth was formed has been, by and large, determined by the amount of carbon dioxide in the air."

"If the volcanic island of Carbonado erupted now, would there be enough carbon dioxide expelled to change the climate?"

"I've calculated that, you know. Were it to erupt now, the gas would mix into the upper air currents and circulate, until it enveloped the globe. It would prevent the diffusion of heat in the lower stratum, as well as heat emanating from the Earth's surface, thus raising the average air temperature some five degrees."

"Professor, can we make it erupt right away?"

"We most likely can. However, the last person up there to do the job will not be able to escape."

"Professor, let me do it! I beg you to tell Chief Engineer Penpen to give his permission."

"There is no way that I can do that. You are still young, and there aren't many others who could do the work that you do."

ところが六月もはじめになって、まだ黄いろなオリザの苗や、芽を出さない樹を見ますと、ブドリはもう居ても立ってもいられませんでした。このままで過ぎるなら、森にも野原にも、ちょうどあの年のブドリの家族のようになる人がたくさんできるのです。ブドリはまるで物も食べずに幾晩も幾晩も考えました。ある晩ブドリは、クーボー大博士のうちを訪ねました。

　「先生、気層のなかに炭酸瓦斯が増えて来れば暖くなるのですか。」

　「それはなるだろう。地球ができてからいままでの気温は、大抵空気中の炭酸瓦斯の量できまっていたと言われる位だからね。」

　「カルボナード火山島が、いま爆発したら、この気候を変える位の炭酸瓦斯を噴くでしょうか。」

　「それは僕も計算した。あれがいま爆発すれば、瓦斯はすぐ大循環の上層の風にまじって地球ぜんたいを包むだろう。そして下層の空気や地表からの熱の放散を防ぎ、地球全体を平均で五度位温にするだろうと思う。」

　「先生、あれを今すぐ噴かせられないでしょうか。」

　「それはできるだろう。けれども、その仕事に行ったもののうち、最後の一人はどうしても遁げられないのでね。」

　「先生、私にそれをやらしてください。どうか先生からペンネン先生へお許しの出るようお詞を下さい。」

　「それはいけない。きみはまだ若いし、いまのきみの仕事に代れるものはそうはない。」

carbon dioxide 「炭酸瓦斯」、二酸化炭素

lower stratum 「下層」（stratum：地層）

"From now on there will be lots of people like me, people who can do anything better than me, people who will accomplish their work far more brilliantly and more beautifully than I can."

"I won't continue discussing this. Bring it up with Chief Engineer Penpen, if you wish."

Budory left and brought up the issue with Chief Engineer Penpen.

"It's a good idea," the chief engineer nodded. "But I'm going to be the one who does it. I'm sixty-three this year. I'm quite content to end my life here and now."

"Sir, but no one knows how it will turn out. It might erupt and the gas might get all soaked up by the rain. It might not go as we think. If you go up there, who will be left to figure out what to do next?"

The old engineer's head drooped down and he fell silent.

Three days after that, the volcano bureau's ship sailed rapidly for Carbonado Island. Several towers were erected on it, and the wires were connected.

When everything was ready, Budory sent everyone else back on the ship, remaining on the island all by himself.

On the next day, the people of Ihatov saw their blue sky cloud to green, and the face of both the sun and moon turn the color of copper.

But, three or four days later, the weather became steadily warmer, and that fall brought a harvest that was almost normal. And countless people who might have had a life just like that of Budory, Neri and their father and mother at the beginning of this story were able to pass that winter happily, with warm food on their tables and bright firewood in their hearths.

「私のようなものは、これから沢山できます。私よりもっともっと何でもできる人が、私よりもっと立派にもっと美しく、仕事をしたり笑ったりして行くのですから。」

「その相談は僕はいかん。ペンネン技師に談(はな)したまえ。」

ブドリは帰って来て、ペンネン技師に相談しました。技師はうなずきました。

「それはいい。けれども僕がやろう。僕は今年もう六十三なのだ。ここで死ぬなら全く本望というものだ。」

「先生、けれどもこの仕事はまだあんまり不確かです。一ぺんうまく爆発しても間もなく瓦斯(がす)が雨にとられてしまうかもしれませんし、また何もかも思った通りいかないかもしれません。先生が今度お出(い)でになってしまっては、あと何とも工夫がつかなくなると存じます。」

老技師はだまって首を垂れてしまいました。

それから三日の後、火山局の船が、カルボナード島へ急いで行きました。そこへいくつものやぐらは建ち、電線は連結されました。

すっかり支度ができると、ブドリはみんなを船で帰してしまって、じぶんは一人島に残りました。

そしてその次の日、イーハトーブの人たちは、青ぞらが緑いろに濁り、日や月が銅(あかがね)いろになったのを見ました。けれどもそれから三四日たちますと、気候はぐんぐん暖かくなってきて、その秋はほぼ普通の作柄になりました。そしてちょうど、このお話のはじまりのようになる筈(はず)の、たくさんのブドリのお父さんやお母さんは、たくさんのブドリやネリといっしょに、その冬を暖かいたべものと、明るい薪(たきぎ)で楽しく暮すことができたのでした。

quite content 「全く本望」、全く満足している

drooped down 「首を垂れて」、うなだれる

bright firewood 「明るい薪」、明るく燃えている薪

hearths いろり

雨ニモマケズ
Strong in the Rain

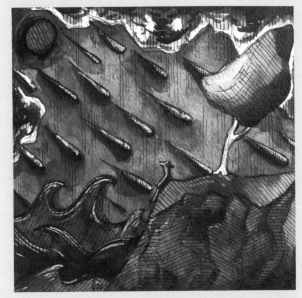

イラスト：ルーシー・パルバース

Strong in the Rain を読むまえに

祈りを込めた静かな笑い

「雨ニモマケズ」という否定形の文の英訳に、なぜ strong という肯定
形の言葉が選ばれているのだろうか。

🔊 **13** *p.174-176*

　1960年代の後半のことでしたが、賢治の弟の宮沢清六さんは、この日本を代表する詩のキーワードは「行ッテ」、すなわち「行く」ことである、と私に言ってくれました。賢治は言葉の達人で言葉をたくみに操る人でしたが、行動こそが人を極楽へと導く媒介物だと確信した作家でもありました。

　「行ッテ」のほかにも注目すべき言葉として「マケズ」があります。「マケズ」には、「屈しない」「くじけない」という意味もあります。そして、この詩の最後の言葉である「ナリタイ」すなわち「ありたい」は、賢治の究極の願望である、世界中の人が「いい人」と判断するような人間になりたいということを語っています。

　しかし、私にとっては、この詩の軸となり、中心となるのは、詩の中盤に入る直前の言葉、

アラユルコトヲ

ジブンヲカンヂャウニイレズニ

ヨクミキキシワカリ

(p.175)

　です。ここで賢治は、自分を顧みず、物事をよく観察し、体験することですべてを理解する人のことを述べています。賢治は10代の頃から敬虔な仏教徒でしたが、真の信仰は信ずることからではなく、自然界の真理を学び、研究することから得られると確信していました。彼の宗教は科学と一体だったのです。

賢治が「マケズ」と否定形を使っているのにもかかわらず、なぜ最初の3行の冒頭の「マケズ」を"strong"と訳したのか、と私は多くの人からと聞かれています。この詩を訳した他の翻訳者の方がたは皆、英訳で否定形を使っているのです。

　ただ、ある言語の、もしくは複数の言語の翻訳者を目指す人ならば、否定的なフレーズは、本質的に反対の意味を持つ形容詞や動詞の肯定形を使ったほうが、よく意味が通るように訳せることが多い、ということを知っておいたほうがよいでしょう。例えば、「(不満が)ない」という意味の「文句がない」は、perfect（完璧な）と訳したほうがよい場合が多いのです。また、飛行機の機内アナウンスでPlease firmly fasten your seat belts.（「シートベルトをしっかり締めてください」）と言われたとき、日本語では「ゆるみのないように、しっかり」と言いますが、これを「ゆるみなく、しっかり」と英訳するのは、この状況下ではおかしいでしょう。

　この詩の英訳では、strongのような一音節の単語がリードすることで、リズムが強化されるのです。清六さんは、賢治が雨に降られることに怯えていたということも私に教えてくれました。賢治は、雨に強い人間に「なりたかった」のです。英訳でstrongを3回繰り返すことで、彼が何を願ったのか、疑いようのない意味をもつ詩になると思います。

　2011年3月、東北地方に地震、津波、原発事故という3つの悲劇

が起きた後、人々は宮沢賢治の作品に救いを求めました。絶望しかない状況の中で、「雨ニモマケズ」は人々が希望を持ち、悲しみを乗り越える力となりました。

　そのことだけでも、宮沢賢治という人が、花巻という小さな町に生まれ、生涯を終えたことに、私たちは感謝すべきでしょう。

賢治の手帳に書かれた「雨ニモマケズ」

Strong in the Rain

Strong in the rain
Strong in the wind
Strong against the summer heat and snow
He is healthy and robust
Free from desire
He never loses his temper
Nor the quiet smile on his lips
He eats four *go* of unpolished rice
Miso and a few vegetables a day
He does not consider himself
In whatever occurs … his understanding
Comes from observation and experience
And he never loses sight of things
He lives in a little thatched-roof hut
In a field in the shadows of a pine tree grove
If there is a sick child in the east
He goes there to nurse the child
If there's a tired mother in the west
He goes to her and carries her sheaves
If someone is near death in the south
He goes and says, "Don't be afraid"
If there are strife and lawsuits in the north
He demands that the people put an end to their pettiness

雨ニモマケズ

雨ニモマケズ

風ニモマケズ

雪ニモ夏ノ暑サニモマケヌ

丈夫ナカラダヲモチ

慾ハナク

決シテ瞋ラズ

イツモシヅカニワラッテヰル

一日ニ玄米四合ト

味噌ト少シノ野菜ヲタベ

アラユルコトヲ

ジブンヲカンヂャウニ入レズニ

ヨクミキキシワカリ

ソシテワスレズ

野原ノ松ノ林ノ蔭ノ

小サナ萱ブキノ小屋ニヰテ

東ニ病気ノコドモアレバ

行ッテ看病シテヤリ

西ニツカレタ母アレバ

行ッテソノ稲ノ束ヲ負ヒ

南ニ死ニサウナ人アレバ

行ッテコハガラナクテモイ、トイヒ

北ニケンクヮヤソショウガアレバ

ツマラナイカラヤメロトイヒ

Free from desire 「慾ハナク」（free from...: ～から逃れて）

never loses his temper 「瞋(いか)ラズ」（lose one's temper: 激怒する）

unpolished rice 「玄米」

In whatever occurs 「アラユルコトヲ」、何が起ころうと

lose sight of... ～を見失う、忘れる

thatched-roof hut 「萱ブキノ小屋」

pine tree grove 「松ノ林」

sheaves （穀物などの）「束」

strife 「ケンクヮ（喧嘩）」、争い、衝突

lawsuits 「ソショウ（訴訟）」

pettiness つまらないこと、些細なこと

He weeps at the time of drought

He plods about at a loss during the cold summer

Everyone calls him Blockhead

No one sings his praises

Or takes him to heart …

That is the kind of person

I want to be

ヒデリノトキハナミダヲナガシ
サムサノナツハオロオロアルキ
ミンナニデクノボートヨバレ
ホメラレモセズ
クニモサレズ
サウイフモノニ
ワタシハナリタイ

drought 「ヒデリ」、干
ばつ
plods 「オロオロアル
キ」、（重い足取りで）とぼ
とぼと歩く
at a loss 途方に暮れて
Blockhead 「デク
ノボー（木偶の坊）」
Takes... to heart 〜を
真剣に受け止める

ロジャー・パルバース
Roger Pulvers

作家、劇作家、演出家、翻訳家、映画監督、東京工業大学名誉教授。1944年、ニューヨークで生まれる。カリフォルニア大学ロサンゼルス校、ハーバード大学大学院卒業。ベトナム戦争への反発からアメリカを離れ、ワルシャワ、パリに留学ののち、1967年に初来日し、京都産業大学、東京工業大学で教鞭をとる。現在はオーストラリア在住。日本に度々帰国している。

　著書には、『星砂物語』（小説：講談社）、『ぼくがアメリカ人をやめたワケ』（大沢章子訳　集英社インターナショナル）、『驚くべき日本語』（早川敦子訳　集英社インターナショナル）など多数。

　宮沢賢治の翻訳・研究者としても知られ、『英語で読む銀河鉄道の夜』（ちくま文庫）、『賢治から、あなたへ　世界はすべてつながっている』（森本奈理訳　集英社インターナショナル）などの著書多数。

宮沢賢治 原文英訳シリーズ2
『セロ弾きのゴーシュ』『注文の多い料理店』を英語で読む

2023年7月10日　第1版第1刷発行

英訳・解説：ロジャー・パルバース

編集協力：熊沢敏之、田中和也、大岩根麻衣、山口西夏

装丁：松本田鶴子

カバー写真：Brett_AdobeStock、Anton Shulgin_AdobeStock
本文イラスト：ルーシー・パルバース

発行人：坂本由子
発行所：コスモピア株式会社
　　　　〒151-0053　東京都渋谷区代々木4-36-4　MCビル2F
営業部：TEL: 03-5302-8378 email: mas@cosmopier.com
編集部：TEL: 03-5302-8379 email: editorial@cosmopier.com

https://www.cosmopier.com/（コスモピア公式ホームページ）
https://e-st.cosmopier.com/（コスモピアeステーション）
https://ebc.cosmopier.com/（子ども英語ブッククラブ）
印刷：シナノ印刷株式会社

本書へのご意見・ご感想をお聞かせください。

本書をお買い上げいただき、誠にありがとうございます。

今後の出版の参考にさせていただきたいので、ぜひ、ご意見・ご感想をお聞かせください。（PC またはスマートフォンで下記のアンケートフォームよりお願いいたします）

アンケートにご協力いただいた方の中から抽選で毎月 10 名の方に、コスモピア・オンラインショップ（https://www.cosmopier.net/）でお使いいただける 500 円のクーポンを差し上げます。（当選メールをもって発表にかえさせていただきます）

https://forms.gle/4geQBovk16VY22Jd8